Getting

RICH

A BEGINNER'S MANUAL

Practical advice to help you to
achieve personal wealth

Getting RICH

A Beginner's Manual

J. H. Brennan

THORSONS PUBLISHING GROUP
Wellingborough, Northamptonshire

First published 1988

© J. H. Brennan 1988

British Library Cataloguing in Publication Data

Brennan, J. H.
Getting rich : a beginner's manual.
1.   Success in business
I.   Title
650. 1   HF5386

ISBN 0-7225-1431-X

Published by Thorsons Publishers Limited, Wellingborough, Northamptonshire, NN8 2RQ, England

Printed in Great Britain by Richard Clay Limited, Bungay, Suffolk

1   3   5   7   9   10   8   6   4   2

CONTENTS

1
THE SECRET OF THE SECOND MILLION

They'll tell you the first million is the hardest, but they never tell you why. In point of fact, that old saying is absolutely true and for good and simple reasons. Those reasons add up to something rich people know and you don't. It's called the Secret of the Second Million. This secret enables them to maintain their living standards and increase their wealth without lifting a finger. As you can imagine, it's a secret worth learning.

The secret of the second million is this:
Once you accumulate wealth to a certain level, the process becomes *automatic*.

This is a very exciting realization. It means you can look forward to a time when you can live and grow richer without working, or planning (or theft!). Your money will have become *self-generating*. At this level, it is no longer difficult to make money. It is, in fact, almost impossible to *stop* making money.

Don't be tempted to dismiss the secret of the second million as simplistic – or, more likely, ignore it on the grounds that it is something so distant from your present circumstances as to be hardly worth bothering about. You know that money makes money. If you have a few pounds in a building society, post office savings or a deposit account with your bank, you will be familiar with the way interest accrues. But accrual of interest is not entirely what the secret of the second million is all about. The real secret is the *level* at which your money begins to self-generate to a worthwhile degree. This level varies from individual to individual, and not one in ten thousand ever bothers to calculate what it is.

Until now.

Your First Investment

In the days when I could still afford the time to play a daily game of penny-ante poker, one of my fellow gamblers had a favourite phrase which he used to encourage the continuation of the game. The phrase was: 'if you don't speculate, you can't accumulate.'

In many ways that's absolutely true. By the time you have finished this book you will hopefully be well equipped to accumulate a great deal. For the moment, however, I want you to speculate. But only a little. I want you to stop reading, head off to the nearest shop and buy yourself a pocket calculator. Nothing fancy, of course. You don't need a very scientific model which can work out the arc cosine of a negative logarithm. And nothing expensive. The last time I looked, you could buy yourself a perfectly adequate calculator for under £10. If you happen to know somebody in the business, you can probably buy one for under £5.

Look upon this purchase not as an indulgence, but as an *investment*. You will certainly be making good use of it very soon indeed. Because armed with your calculator and the information in this chapter, you are going to make some vital calculations. By the time you have finished, you will know the secret of the second million *as it applies to you*.

Your Survival Threshold

The air you breathe comes free. After that, it's money all the way. Just how much money can be a revelation.

Very few of us ever sit down and calculate how much it costs to live the way we do. We pay our bills when we have to, tighten our belts before pay-day and binge a little afterwards.

So long as we (somehow!) keep within our income and our overdraft, we tend to leave the frightening financial details alone. This is all very well if the only thing you want is a quiet life. But if you want to be rich, you had better get comfortable with financial calculations.

What comes next is one of the most fundamental financial calculations you will ever make: your personal cost of living. To help you with it, I've asked an expert accountant to list some of the many, many ways in which you might be spending your money. That list is printed on the following pages.

After each entry, you will find a blank space to fill in. This is where you enter how much *you* spend on the item listed. Your answer could be a zero or £10,000. Don't guess. Check out each answer. It's a nuisance, but you are laying the foundations of future wealth, so it will be time well spent.

Once you have worked out the accurate figure, write it down. What we are ultimately looking for in every case is how much you spend under the heading listed *in a calendar year*. It is important that all your figures refer to a year, otherwise your final total will be inaccurate. In many instances, this will mean converting information you have to hand. Mortgage payments, for example, are normally made monthly. Where I live, phone bills are paid quarterly. And so on.

It is not difficult to convert figures like these into yearly totals *but remember to do it*. Even professionals sometimes forget.

Once you have finished figuring out how much you spend under each heading, use your calculator to add them all together. The final figure will be your personal cost of living: the amount of money it takes to keep you alive and functioning at your present living standard on this planet for one year.

When you reach that stage, I want to promise you two things. One is that you have just completed the hardest part of the personal get-rich programme built into this book. The other is that you have laid a solid foundtion for what is to come. But more of that later. For now, let's get down to figuring.

2
THE PERSONAL COST OF LIVING

How to complete this section

What we're looking for is how much it costs you to exist at your present standard of living for one year. But most of your money won't be spent on an annual basis. If you smoke cigarettes, for example, the chances are you buy a pack *each day*. If you run a car, you probably buy petrol once or twice a *week*. And so on.

To make things easy, I've laid out this section in columns under the headings: Daily, Bi-weekly (i.e. twice a week), Weekly, Fortnightly (i.e., every two weeks), Monthly, Quarterly, and Yearly.

Against each item you should first list the money you spend *under the most convenient heading*. If you spend £2 a day on cigarettes, list that under the Daily column. If petrol costs you £10 a week, that cost goes under the Weekly column. And so on. However you spend it, that's where you should list it. (Although most are fairly obvious, some of those items need a little explanation. If you get confused while filling in, turn to the **Help Section** on page 12. Most of the explanations you need will be in there.)

Immediately after you have made each entry in its most natural and convenient form, convert it into a yearly figure and enter that in the Yearly column on the extreme right. This is where your new calculator can come in handy, even though the formulae are very simple. To convert quarterly to yearly, multiply by 4; monthly to yearly, multiply by 12; fornightly to yearly, multiply by 26; weekly to yearly, multiply by 52; bi-weekly to yearly, multiply by 104; and daily to yearly, multiply by 365.

Finally, when you have everything filled in and converted to Yearly totals in each case, add together all those Yearly totals. The final figure you reach is your Personal Cost of Living. I'm betting at this stage it will come as something of a surprise to you.

Help Section

Just to make absolutely sure you know exactly what everything means, here is an explanation of each of those items.

Cash. Your spending money. The sort that just disappears and you don't even know where it's gone.

Groceries. Include all domestic items (detergent, light bulbs, loo rolls), not just food.

Lunch. If your work or lifestyle means you eat lunch away from home, insert cost against this heading.

Restaurant. This covers more formal (and usually more expensive!) eating out.

Mortgage. If you *rent* your house of flat, you should still use this heading to list your outgoings.

Heat. Whether it's a coal fire, an electric heater or full central heating, it all costs.

Gas. For cooking – unless you use electricity.

Electricity. For cooking – unless you use gas.

Water. This may not be as free as you imagine. Most, if not all local authorities charge water rates. Even if you have your own well, it costs to pump the stuff.

	Daily ×365	Bi-weekly ×104	Weekly ×52	Fortnightly ×26	Monthly ×12	Quarterly ×4	YEARLY
CASH							
GROCERIES							
LUNCH							
RESTAURANT							
MORTGAGE							
HEAT							
GAS							
ELECTRICITY							
WATER							
TELEPHONE							
CLOTHES							
ACCESSORIES							

	Daily ×365	Bi-weekly ×104	Weekly ×52	Fortnightly ×26	Monthly ×12	Quarterly ×4	YEARLY
CAR							
REPAYMENTS							
ROAD TAX							
INSURANCE							
DEPRECIATION							
MAINTENANCE							
REPAIRS							
PETROL							
GARAGE FEES							
PARKING FEES							
INSURANCE:							
LIFE							
HOUSEHOLD							
SPECIAL							

	Daily ×365	Bi-weekly ×104	Weekly ×52	Fortnightly ×26	Monthly ×12	Quarterly ×4	YEARLY
ENTERTAINMENT							
HOLIDAYS							
DOCTOR							
DENTIST							
OPTICIAN							
CHIROPODIST							
SPECIALIST							
PHARMACY							
CHARITY							
POLITICAL PARTY							
GIFTS							
HAIRDRESSER							

	Daily ×365	Bi-weekly ×104	Weekly ×52	Fortnightly ×26	Monthly ×12	Quarterly ×4	YEARLY
COMPUTER							
INCOME TAX							
INTEREST							
REPAYMENTS:							
BANK CHARGES							
HIRE PURCHASE							
TERM LOAN							
OVERDRAFT							
DEPENDANTS							
CHRISTMAS							
SAVINGS							
CLUB							
CONTRIBUTIONS							

	Daily ×365	Bi-weekly ×104	Weekly ×52	Fortnightly ×26	Monthly ×12	Quarterly ×4	YEARLY
POSTAGE							
ACCOUNTANT							
LEGAL EXPENSES							
PIANO TUNER							
CREDIT CARDS:							
VISA							
ACCESS							
AMERICAN EXPRESS							
DINER'S CLUB							
OTHER							
HOBBY							
CIGARETTES							

	Daily ×365	Bi-weekly ×104	Weekly ×52	Fortnightly ×26	Monthly ×12	Quarterly ×4	YEARLY
CIGARS							
TOBACCO							
SWEETS							
NEWSPAPERS							
BOOKS							
PETS							
MISCELLANEOUS							
OTHER							

Telephone. Your phone always costs far more than you imagine. Check the bills.

Clothes. You may believe you haven't a thing to wear, but you certainly aren't running around naked. Calculate carefully how much you spend on clothes over the year from underwear to overcoat; and don't forget shoes, which come into this category.

Accessories. This is a broad category to cover everything you wear that isn't clothes. Earrings fall into this category. So do watches.

Car repayments. This would include lease or rental charges where appropriate. If you own your car outright, this section is left blank, but be sure to put a figure under **depreciation**, which is explained below.

Car road tax. The money you pay the Government to dig pot-holes in your area.

Car insurance. You probably pay this on an annual basis, but if the cost is spread, remember this usually involves an interest charge on top of your annual premium.

Car depreciation. If you own your car outright (and even if you don't) it still loses value each year. A chat with your local car salesperson will give you an indication of how much.

Car maintenance. In this context, the cost of servicing.

Car repairs. Cost of breakdowns and crashes both come into this category.

Petrol. This cost used to be fairly consistent. Now it tends to fluctuate. If you are in real difficulty, average out what you spend.

Garage fees. The cost (if any) of keeping your car off the streets at night.

Parking fees. The cost of feeding the meter (and paying the fine when you don't.)

Life insurance. Don't worry about trying to calculate how much you get back on an endowment policy. For the purposes of this exercise, just tot up your annual premium.

Household insurance. You may or may not have it. If you do, what is the annual premium?

Special insurance. Again, you may or may not have it. My stepson, who is a photographer, has special insurance on his camera equipment. I have special insurance on some computer gear. If you have any insurance which lies outside the more usual categories of car, life and household, list the cost here.

Entertainment. This is a broad category which would cover everything from a pint at your local to a night at the opera, including hire of dress suit.

Holidays. I haven't managed a holiday in five years. You may be luckier; but this is where you count the cost.

Doctor. If you are ever sick, getting well costs. Base your calculations on what you spent last year. If you had a once-only hospital treatment (like an appendix operation, which by definition can't be done twice) don't take any cost incurred into your annual calculation unless you are paying off a loan engendered by it. If you anticipate any major surgery in coming years, cost in one-fifth of what you expect to pay out. Don't forget, even the British National Health Service will not absolutely guarantee that ill-health comes free. Most of us buy a new nightie or pyjamas when admitted to hospital!

Dentist. Those gold fillings may be an investment, but what did you pay for the privilege?

Optician. If you have poor eyesight, you will probably consult an optician once every two years. Divide by two to find your annual outgoing.

Chiropodist. I doubt if someone with beautiful feet like yours would spend much money here, but you never know.

Specialist. Any medical practitioner, surgeon, anaesthetist, healer, bone-setter, acupuncturist, chiropractor, witch-doctor etc. not covered above.

Pharmacy. A visit to the doctor often results in separate charges for drugs from your neighbourhood pharmacy.

Charity. Charitable donations may be tax deductible, but you still have to find the money to make them in the first place.

Political party. Dues, gifts or expenses.

Gifts. Christmas and birthdays are a drain on resources which is seldom accurately calculated . . . until now.

Hairdresser. Or barber.

Computer. A very great many people now own a computer, to judge from sales statistics. And computers can cost vast sums of money to run, however little electricity they consume. I have two that are eating me out of house and home. If you have one or more, count the cost of software, periferals, floppies, cables, communications and so on.

Income tax. Unless you are very clever, very lucky or very crooked, you probably have to pay at least some.

Bank charges. It costs you to run a bank account. It costs you more to run it in the red.

Hire purchase. Accountants get very clever about HP and other loans (see below), often insisting that you really should calculate only the interest on the loan as an outgoing since the value of the item you bought is shown as a credit on your balance books. Since we are not carrying out an audit, but merely trying to find out how much you need to survive, you can ignore this and record how much you pay back in a year without differentiating between capital and interest.

Term loan. See above.

Overdraft. See above and remember that overdraft charges are apt to slip past unnoticed.

Dependants. If love or duty persuades you to support (an) other human being(s), then the cost of providing that support forms part of your personal cost of living.

Christmas savings. If you enter under this category, make sure you don't duplicate the same expenditure under gifts.

Club. Dues and expenses. Remember, sporting clubs often involve the purchase or hire of sporting equipment.

Contributions. A catch-all heading for regular donations to institutions or organizations not already mentioned.

Postage. You know how much the stamp costs: don't forget the envelope costs too.

Accountant. If you have someone doing your books, (s)he will charge you money to tell you how broke you are.

Legal expenses. If you are stuck with ongoing legal expenses, this one is simple to calculate. If you had legal expenses last year which seem unlikely to recur, write in one-fifth as a rule of thumb for your present calculation.

Piano tuner. If you have a piano and an ear for music, you should pay out under this heading at least once a year.

Credit cards. Once again, we're looking for the average sums these addictive little monsters persuade you to spend each year, *not* simply the interest which undoubtedly accrues through using some of them. Don't forget to calculate in the charge for the card itself where this is applicable.

Hobby. Even if it's only origami, the chances are it will cost you something.

Cigarettes/cigars/tobacco. Think before you calculate this one. The chances are you pretend to yourself you smoke a little less than you actually do.

Sweets. You pay for the privilege of rotting your teeth.

Newspapers. If you're over 40, you probably still think of your newspaper as costing you a few pence per week. Take a deep breath and look at the cover price. Now.

Books. This book cost you money. So will all the others you will buy during the year.

Pets. Work out the cost of food, licence where appropriate and any special equipment which arises out of keeping your particular pet.

Miscellaneous. Incidental expenses that don't fall into the categories already listed.

Other. Anything you forgot to list under Miscellaneous.
If you've followed the instructions so far, you should now be looking at a figure which represents the cost of living on Earth for one year at your present standard. If you discover (as you undoubtedly will) that this figure is higher than your annual income, don't panic unduly. The amount you owe now is only a problem while you remain poor. Once you get rich, you can owe millions and still enjoy a good night's sleep.

But before you start to apply the Secret of the Second Million to that figure, ask yourself a question. If you were wealthy now, would you still live the way you do?

The chances are the answer to that question is no. If you were rich you would drive a better car, live in a bigger house (maybe even in a different country). You might want to eat out more often, substitute the odd plate of caviar for your current diet of chip butties. You would dress more fashionably, have your hair styled more often. And so on. In other words, your Personal Cost of Living would *go up*.

This is where you have to make an educated guess about your new lifestyle—the lifestyle you will have when you apply the lessons in this book and end up rich. You have to guess how much that lifestyle is going to cost *in relation to your present outgoings*. Do you imagine it will cost you twice as much? Three times? Ten times? This isn't a quiz and there are no right and wrong answers. You are the only person who can supply the final figure. Money changes the way some people live a great deal. With others you'd hardly notice the difference. Calculating your current Personal Cost of Living has given you some very real insights into where the money actually disappears to; and you should use these insights to make a sensible evaluation of the annual figure you think would support you in the style to which you wish to become accustomed.

Just for fun, write down your estimate here:

£_____.____

You now have two important figures. One, which should be very accurate, represents the money you spend to maintain your present standard of living. The other, admittedly a guesstimate, represents the money you think you would have to spend in order to live the way you want to. Let's see how the Secret of the Second Million applies to these figures.

The Money Tree

If you keep £100 in a sock underneath your mattress, it will remain £100 for as long as you're prepared to leave it there. If, however, you deposit that £100 in a bank or building society, it will grow just like a tree because the financial institution concerned will credit your account with *interest*.

There are two main types of interest—simple and compound. Let's suppose the bank agrees to pay you 10 per cent per annum on your £100. At the end of the first year, the *simple interest* accrued would amount to £10, which you might then withdraw and spend on champagne and high living. At the end of the second year, your £100 would have generated another £10 interest for you to spend in a similar manner.

But if you happen to be a teetotal recluse, you might decide not to withdraw the £10 simple interest, credited to your account at the end of the first year. This means that in the second year the bank would have to pay you 10 per cent on £110 and not just £100. Thus at the end of the second year, simple interest on your deposit would amount to £11, not £10. Looking at your investment over the two years, you would find that the interest your money earned amounted to £21. This figure is called *compound* interest.

I can't imagine why you would find this explanation of compound interest confusing, but if you did, don't worry. Our Secret of the Second Million calculation will be based on simple interest only. The formula for the Secret of the Second Million runs like this:

Current (or anticipated) cost of living divided by interest rate percentage and the result multiplied by 100 equals money needed.

Like most formulae, this one seems complicated at first sight. An example run will make it clearer.

Let's suppose, to pull a figure out of the air, that it costs you £15,000 a year to live the way you do now. Let's further suppose that when you enquire about bank interest rates, you find they're running at 8 per cent. Applying our formula, we divide £15,000 by 8, which gives us £1,875. Then we multiply our answer by 100, which gives us £187,500.

In other words, if you happened to have exactly £187,500 to put on deposit in your bank right now, it would allow you to live at the rate of £15,000 a year for as long as the 8 per cent interest rate held up.

Now we'll take it a step further. If you assume that your *projected* lifestyle (the way you'd like to live when you get rich) is going to cost you, say, £250,000 a year, the figures work out like this;

£250,000 divided by 8 equals £31,250. Multiply this by 100 and you find you need £3,125,000 on deposit to keep you going without work or effort.

Now you've seen how it's done, substitute your own figures and the current bank interest rate to find out at what level your money will become self-perpetuating—because, of course, every pound you have on deposit *above* the figure needed to maintain your lifestyle makes you *additional money* which you will not spend. This additional money then accrues *compound interest* as we demonstrated earlier, making you richer still with no work or effort.

I would be the first to admit that the examples I've just given you are simplistic. It is, for example, highly unlikely that you would settle for the standard bank deposit rate if you had three million pounds to invest. But we are not preparing an audit or planning an investment portfolio here. What we are doing is showing you how to work out your *first financial goal*. Once you have grasped the principle—which is really very easy to understand—you can refine the final figure as much as you wish. The important thing is that you end up with a figure which represents your personal financial goal.

Knowing your personal financial goal is important. Most people vaguely think they would like to have a lot of money. Some people are even prepared to work very hard in order to accumulate a lot of money. But very few people actually know *how much* money they really need in order to live the way they want to without work or effort.

It is precisely those very few people who have far and away the greatest chance of succeeding in the quest to get rich.

And in case you haven't noticed, you've just joined them.

3
THE MIDAS SYNDROME

Your mother knew how you could get rich. Take care of the pennies, your mother told you, and the pounds will take care of themselves. Your mother was wrong. That old saying of hers will never make you rich, although it will certainly stop you getting poor—which is not, however, the same thing.

Good money management starts with the pennies, as your mother was very well aware. A few years ago, a British bank ran an advertising campaign with guidelines about living within your means. It was aimed at people who consistently spent more than they earned, who sank deeper into debt, who just couldn't seem to balance their personal budget.

If that sounds like you, you may be interested to hear the first and most important piece of advice issued by that bank. The advice was: Stop cashing *small* cheques.

That's a bit of a stopper when you first see it. Surely if anybody gets into debt, it's by cashing *large* cheques. Not so, says the bank. You're very aware of what you're doing when you write a large cheque. You think about it and worry about it and remember it. You *almost always* write it for a *specific purpose*—you're buying a house or a car or paying for your holiday. Because the whole operation is so visible, large cheques tend to fall squarely within your budget. You're scared to let them fall anywhere else.

Writing small cheques is different. Your mind switches to automatic. You write them without thinking. You forget about them. *Cashing* small cheques is even worse. If you write a small cheque to buy yourself a pair of sunglasses, at least you have the sunglasses to remind you that you wrote the cheque. If you write a small cheque for *cash*, I can guarantee that within a day or two (maybe less) you won't have a hint of a reminder left. The cash will have gone, the cheque will have gone and the memory will have gone. Before you know it, you're writing another small cheque.

The problem with small cheques is that they mount up. Before you know it, they mount up so much that they nudge you over that magic boundary which indicates where you start living beyond your means. That's why the bank advised you to stop cashing small cheques. Take care of the pennies, as Mother told you, and the pounds will take care of themselves. Good advice from your mother, good advice from the Bank, but not relevant at all to getting rich. Have you ever heard of anybody who made a million by *saving*?

F. Scott Fitzgerald, the Poet Laureate of the Jazz Age, remarked that the very rich are different from you and me. He was wrong too, but more subtly. The rich certainly *seem* different. But what sets them apart is quite superficial and capable of duplication.

What *does* set the rich apart?

They usually dress better. Even leaving aside the designer labels, their clothes have that elusive aura of cut and quality which suggests money. They tend to drive larger cars and live in larger houses. Their hands are manicured, their skin is tanned (even in winter), their hair is styled. Even today they may have servants. They have certain habits (like not bothering to ask the price) certain gestures, certain attitudes which mark them out. I call the totality of these attributes, from clothes to gestures, the *Midas Syndrome*. It is something you should know much more about.

Prosperism

Have you ever noticed how people often differ when they

describe someone; even someone they know extremely well? An individual may be described as cruel and kind, gentle and aggressive, religious and profane. In less extreme cases, one person may talk of an individual's interest in sport while another remains utterly unaware of it.

Some of the discrepancies might be explained by poor observation, but this hardly holds good for glaring contradictions. One has to assume some other factor is at work: and it is. Once your attention is drawn to the puzzle, observation soon supplies the answer. It is an answer, however, which I have never seen discussed in any of the standard textbooks on psychology. Hence, for convenience, I intend to call it *prosperism*.

Prosperism is defined as the stimulation of certain characteristics and responses in other people. As Prospero, in Shakespeare's *The Tempest*, was reputed to be able to call up spirits from the vasty deep, so most of us seem able to call up aspects of another's personality which may well be hidden from others.

All too often, of course, we may remain blissfully unaware of what we are doing. Consequently, we misinterpret the nature of prosperism. We consider ourselves 'unlucky' because so many people swindle us. We feel irritated because so many women want to mother us. We look for answers in the world outside and never consider that we ourselves have a responsibility for generating such attitudes.

Sociologists have long been aware of the curious fact that battered wives were often also battered children. What this means is difficult to evaluate. Perhaps the violence of parents (usually the father) taught the child responses which called up similar violence in others. Or perhaps the responses were innate, calling up violence in father and husband alike. That the element of prosperism is valid, is underlined by the fact that all too often a battered wife who manages to break away from her vicious husband, will subsequently form a relationship with another man who quickly proves equally violent.

Once you are alerted to the nature of prosperism, you can see it everywhere; and nowhere more clearly, perhaps, than in your own responses. You will, of course, have met people whom you disliked on sight—with no apparent reason. Doubtless you have friends who make you feel good without saying a word. You may know someone in whom you instinctively confide; and others who make you feel uncomfortable, suspicious, even paranoid. In every case, these people are *calling up* something from the deeper layers of your psyche, just as you are doubtless *calling up* specific aspects of their personality.

The Laws of Prosperism

But if prosperism exists, what are the laws which govern it? The bottom line answer seems to be that we do not know; at least, not entirely. But there are certainly some prosperism factors which may be analysed out and some which we seem to grasp instinctively.

On this latter point, you may like to cast your mind back to the last time you went to a job interview. The chances are you groomed yourself with special care and put on your best clothes. Why? You may tell yourself, truthfully enough, that you wanted to create a good impression. But if you think about your motivation carefully, you will realize that you actually hoped to *generate a favourable response*. Which is another way of saying you wanted to call up a benevolent aspect from your interviewer's personality: in short, prosperism.

From this, we may deduce that *appearance* influences prosperism. But this may go beyond the good suit you put on for a job interview or the way you do your hair. Your physical appearance—those aspects of it which lie beyond dress and grooming—can be an instrument which calls up prosperic reactions. And here we may have a clue to one of the dynamics of prosperism.

Several years ago a work colleague of mine was introduced to a new junior manager in the company and reacted with such immediate dislike that he was literally gasping for breath before he got himself under control. The young manager was faultless in this exchange and it is to be hoped he was unaware of my colleague's reaction. But my colleague himself was profoundly disturbed. He recognized that his reaction had been totally irrational and spent some considerable time in self-examination, attempting to discover where it had come from. Eventually he succeeded. The manager reminded him of an old rival: not in dress, manner or appearance, but in voice. The linkage was quite unconscious at their first encounter, but unconscious or not, it was sufficiently strong to call up a very negative response.

One wonders how far our failures and successes are determined by the responses our appearance, voice, subtle body scents or mannerisms may call up in others by reminding them unconsciously of old enemies or friends. Yet I cannot believe *all* prosperism is the result of such half-buried recollections. Indeed, I am certain another aspect of it is fundamentally biological.

Learning from Animals

A dogfight is a spectacular performance, though it usually upsets the owners of the pets far more than the dogs involved. Even catfights, which are substantially more vicious when they take place between two toms, seldom end in the death or serious mutilation of either participant. Nor is this peculiarity confined to domestic animals. Throughout the wild, intra-species conflicts (over territory, mates or food) seldom result in serious damage to the participants. The reason for this, as zoologists have long been aware, is that much animal behaviour is rigidly conditioned by a code of signals; and nowhere are such codes more evident than in a conflict situation.

The reason why the victor in a dogfight does not kill his vanquished opponent is that, invariably, the loser will have given the submission signal: he will have rolled on his back and offered his unprotected throat. In such circumstances, the victor, far from going for the jugular, will lose interest in the fight and walk away. Not only may fights be stopped by the submission signal, they may actually be avoided in the same way. This signal and many others—the sexual display of birds, the paralysing scream of the predator—seem to be part of an evolutionary system designed to call up specific, biologically programmed responses. Such responses are quite involuntary and sometimes downright dangerous, as when a prey animal freezes at the scream of a hunter. They are also obviously very difficult to suppress.

Humans are, of course, part of the animal kingdom, so it is not outlandish to suggest that we too may have certain biological responses programmed in. If so, this biological programming may explain certain near-universal reactions to specific personality types. Dickens's famous Uriah Heep exhibited characteristics which were, at face value, praiseworthy. He was modest, unassuming and careful to tread on no one's toes. Yet in combination, these same characteristics create loathing in most of us. Individuals who cringe call up impatient aggression, as if they had invisible KICK ME notices pinned to their backs.

In this context, we may refer back to the world of animals to discover that by far the most important biological signal systems are related to the hierarchy of *power*. If you are, let us suppose, a young buffalo, it is vitally important that you know your place in the scheme of things. If you do not, you are liable to fall foul of your betters, usurping their best grazing, for example, or trying, in season, to mate with the leader's harem.

Such mistakes can be costly. They lead to banishment from the herd or fights to the death: situations you would do well to avoid if at all possible. And, though it is less obvious, they are situations which the *herd* would do well to avoid if at all possible since they lead to a diminuation of total strength and are ultimately counter-survival.

The example given is masculine, but female societies have their own rigid structures as well. The term *pecking order* arose from actual observation of hens: the top hen is allowed to peck the lesser hens, but they are not allowed to peck back.

In order to preserve the status quo without the weakening effect of endless bloodshed, Nature has developed a series of subtle signals by which most species may recognize their dominant members. Such signals are exchanged and acted upon at a totally instinctive level. The young bulls avoid upsetting the leader of the herd, at least until such time as they imagine they are strong enough to take his place. Interestingly, the same signals are picked up by the young cows, who will mate far more willingly with a dominant bull than with any of the lesser lights. And though it is less often remarked upon by our chauvinist zoologists, the reverse also seems to be true, suggesting dominance ranking is just as prevalent, if slightly less obvious, among the female of the species.

Despite our best attempts to root them out through various political philosophies, dominance structures twist like taproots through every human culture. Even in Communist countries, as Orwell pointed out, some are more equal than others. The cream in any culture is composed of the rich and powerful: and in most cultures, the terms *rich* and *powerful* are virtually synonymous.

All this is obvious enough. What is less obvious is that the rich and powerful of the human species exhibit exactly the same characteristics as their dominant counterparts in the buffalo herd or the chicken-run or the wolf pack: they signal their status. And the signals are picked up and acted upon, instinctively, by other members of the species.

The exchange of signals, the conditioned interaction, is as easily observed among humans as it is in the wild. The millionaire engenders deference far beyond his common-sense entitlement. His or her opinion weighs heavily even on subjects for which (s)he has no qualifications. One is always cautious not to upset the very wealthy, just as the young bull is cautious not to upset the leader of the herd. That wealth adds to sexual attraction, exactly as dominance does in the wild, is beyond dispute. The (apparently) ugly old male millionaire with his stunningly attractive young wife has become a social cliché. And wealthy women are attractive too—and not only to gigolos after their money.

This then, in its totality, is the Midas Syndrome: the collection of obvious attributes and subtle signals which mark out an individual as wealthy and *call up instinctive responses in others*. It is that calling up, that prosperism, which is important in the present context, for it is the key to turning the whole Midas Syndrome into a powerful tool to help you make it to the top.

Midas Benefits

The rich get rich and the poor get children, as the old song tells us. We already know one of the reasons why the rich get rich: as we noted earlier, the Secret of the Second Million is at work for them. But this is not the only reason why the rich get rich. Another reason, equally important, is that there is a *cultural conspiracy* to aid them on their way to greater heights. And it is, in my view, a conspiracy based firmly on the Midas Syndrome.

When individuals become rich, they are treated differently from the remainder of the herd. The reactions of those around them are instinctively related to their exalted status. In business, they are offered the top jobs and the top salaries. Often their prestige is sufficiently high to earn them psuedo-work, boardroom appointments which carry large stipends but involve no actual responsibilities.

The Utopian principle *To each according to his needs, from each according to his abilities* is absolutely alien to the way in which, typically, we treat the very rich. Tradespeople offer them special discounts in order to encourage their continued custom. They benefit from extended credit; and are seldom too severely harassed if they step beyond permitted bounds.

What do you give the man who has everything? The answer, inevitably, is something expensive. And to the rich, gifts are far from rare: there is always somebody who wishes to curry favour or express appreciation in tangible form.

These are very real benefits. Cumulatively, they can have quite as much influence on the growth of individual wealth as the Secret of the Second Million. But unlike the Secret of the Second Million, the Midas Syndrome comes into play at a relatively early stage. You will begin to project success long before you become a literal millionaire; and the subtle signals will provoke a beneficial response. You will find you no longer have to argue quite so hard for your next pay rise. You will find your clients no longer argue when you fix a fee. There will come a time when you can safely leave others to evaluate your worth; and enjoy the pleasant surprise of discovering they are prepared to pay you more (sometimes much more) than you would normally have asked to do the job.

Like the Secret of the Second Million, your personal development of the Midas Syndrome is something you can look forward to with pleasurable anticipation. But the good news is that you won't have to wait nearly so long as you may imagine, because you can consciously *develop* the Midas Syndrome long before you actually get rich.

Making a Midas

One morning not so long ago, I called unexpectedly at the home of a friend to discover him immaculately dressed, impeccably shaved, well groomed, manicured and humming a jaunty little tune.

'How do I look?' he asked me promptly.

'Great!' I told him truthfully.

'Would you say I look like a million dollars?'

'Yes, I would,' I said.

'Good,' he told me. 'That's how much I'm trying to borrow.'

He was a man who knew the power of the Midas Syndrome. It is a matter of common observation that bankers will never lend you money unless you don't need it. In other words, you have to be rich to get a loan. What a great many people miss, however, is the fact that your financial status is often more a matter of judgement than fact. If the banker only *thinks* you're rich, the end result remains the same.

This was the game my friend was playing, of course. He instinctively recognized that in order to borrow a million, he had to look worth that sort of money. Hence the expensive suit and the barber-shop shave.

But his efforts went far beyond these superficial factors. The car he drove was a prestige Jaguar. The briefcase he carried was a handmade slimline pigskin. The watch on his wrist was a Swiss analogue in a solid gold case. Beyond immediate appearances, he had a business address in the most desirable commercial quarter of the city. The appointment with his bankers had been made, not by himself, but by his secretary who had mentioned smoothly that he would soon be returning from the signing of an important contract in Geneva. In all this, of course, he was sending out Midas signals. But the most important signals of all were personal. He was relaxed, confident, articulate. He took the lead in conversations. He selected quality as if by instinct. He did not ask the price.

These subtle personal signals are, if anything, even more important than physical appearances. You have doubtless met many a man on his way to a wedding in his impeccable hired suit from Moss Bros. He looks great and is stepping from an expensive limousine, but you would never mistake him for a millionaire, simply because his attitudes are wrong. He looks out of place, vaguely uncomfortable in the suit, talks about the wrong things in the wrong way and defers to those around him as the wealthy never do.

Conversely, I can recall a day many years ago when my wife and I called at a stately home in Ireland and were approached across the lawn by a man we took, at a distance, to be the gardener. He was dressed in tattered work clothes and there was earth beneath his fingernails. But as he came closer, it was immediately obvious this was no paid employee. All the signals were wrong, from the way he held himself to the way he spoke. He was, in fact, the owner of the manor.

It is important to realize two things about the Midas Syndrome. The first is that the superficial aspects can be *faked*. The second is that the subtle signals may be *developed*.

Fakery is easy. We live in a credit-based society so that acceptably well-cut clothes may be had today and paid for, in instalments, tomorrow. If you prefer not to sink into debt before coming rich, you can always search the jumble sales for exclusive labels and sew them onto less imposing garments. Cars may be leased or hired, a spouse press-ganged into playing the role of private secretary or personal assistant. And so on. Unless you are flat broke, you will find if you are honest with yourself that keeping up a Midas appearance is largely a matter of priorities. Deny yourself a holiday this year and you not only have more to spend on clothes, but you have instantly generated two or more additional weeks earning time. Have fewer nights out, abandon your hobby, stop smoking or drinking—you know by now the areas in which you spend your money (another reason for the financial exercise in Chapter 1) and consequently you know what priorities have to be changed in order to bring your appearance more in line with the Midas Syndrome.

Subtle signals, however, cannot be bought on credit. They arise out of an inner state which comes with power and money, but which can be successfully nurtured without either. The nurturing process is a little complicated, however, and warrants a chapter all to itself.

4
SUCCESS SIGNALS

When I prepared the outline for this book, I promised the publishers a severely practical work with none of the curious mental gymnastics found in so many other self-improvement manuals. Now, no further in than Chapter 4, I am about to break that promise. But perhaps I can make it a short chapter to compensate.

If you feel shy, you blush. If you feel happy, you smile. And if you feel rich and powerful a whole host of flags are flying in the form of posture, gesture, tonal quality, scent and heaven knows what else. Actors are particularly aware of such signals and incorporate some of them into their performances to enhance characterization. Method actors go further (whether they know it or not) and attempt to incorporate *all* of them.

Method acting attracted a great deal of publicity in the 1950s and 1960s, probably because it sounded so bizarre. Method actors were taught to adopt a role so completely that they *became* the character. *En route* to this ideal, they engaged in exercises during which they imagined themselves to be birds or animals or even vegetable entities like a tree. This sort of thing is always good for a media laugh, but the amusement abated when it became clear that the approach was capable of producing some very fine actors.

Method acting is based on the premise that the signals you send out depend on how you feel inside; and that how you feel inside can be changed by the application of imagination. Thus, if you wish to play a villain, it no longer becomes necessary to remember all the postures and gestures associated with villainy. You *imagine* yourself a villain instead and the signals are sent out automatically.

You are not, presumably, an actor, but this approach will still work for you if you are prepared to invest a little time and effort. Not only will it generate the Midas signals automatically, but it will, if you persevere, bring you an interesting package of side benefits, including increased self-confidence, greater relaxation and a generally sunny disposition.

If method acting works because the way you feel conditions the signals you send out, long-term benefits accrue because of the structure of the human mind.

Unless you are totally disinterested in psychology, you will be aware that your mind is broadly divided into two important aspects: the conscious and the unconscious. In very simple terms, the conscious mind determines what you *do*, the unconscious what you *feel*. When you begin to use your imagination in a certain way, you are, in effect, sending a message to the unconscious telling it how you *want* to feel. And the unconscious will respond by delivering the goods—provided, that is, you send the message when you are totally relaxed.

It's not all that easy to communicate with your own unconscious. There is a barrier to get over. (Psychologists reckon this barrier is necessary to prevent unconscious contents erupting like lava and overpowering the conscious.) But the barrier is not raised all the time. It disappears completely in sleep, for example, and you are able to enjoy that incredible 3-D participation picture show we call dreaming. It also drops, for reasons I don't pretend to understand, when you relax. And the more you relax, the more it drops.

Bell, Book and Canine

Pavlov, a founding father of modern psychological thought, became famous for his conditioning experiments with dogs. In simple terms, what Pavlov did was to ring a bell each time he presented a hungry dog with meat. When the dog saw the meat, its mouth watered. After a while, Pavlov rang the bell without producing the meat. The dog's mouth still watered. Pavlov concluded the animal's salivary reflex had become conditional on the bell rather than the meat. When his report of the experiments went into English, a small mistake in translation changed 'conditional reflex' to *conditioned reflex* and the term stuck.

Salivation isn't the only reflex you can condition, of course. If you are prepared to invest the time, virtually any physical and quite a few psychological functions can be controlled using Pavlovian techniques. And that includes the tension reflexes associated with stress.

If, like Pavlov, you ring a bell next time you give your dog his dinner, you will swiftly discover a conditioned reflex is not an instant occurrence. It is something which builds up with time and requires a whole series of repetitions to establish. When you talk about conditioning, you talk about something very similar to *training*.

I have worked out a course to help you send out automatic Midas signals. It is based partly on the Stanislavski Method, partly on Pavlovian conditioning. It is a course which starts by teaching you how to relax, and is run for *at least* three months in order to ensure the conditioning aspects lock in properly.

On this latter point, it is important—indeed vital—that you practise the exercises *every day*. They will only take about twenty minutes of your time, but that daily twenty minutes will work whereas far longer periods at irregular intervals will generate no results at all.   On which minor warning note, let us now get on with . . .

The Relaxing 3-Month Think-Rich Midas Signals Course

Week 1
This week you are going to learn the art and practice of

relaxation. The exercise is absolutely fundamental to everything else which follows.

Learning about relaxation begins, oddly enough, with learning about tension. The reason for this is that most of us are blissfully unaware of how tense we are. We race through our day with hunched shoulders, gritted teeth and rigid abdomens and when someone mentions tension, we looked surprised and say, 'What me?'

Before you can even begin to relax, you need to know at a conscious level what physical, muscular tension actually feels like. In other words, you must begin by experiencing your tensions *at a conscious level*.

Set aside half an hour each morning. (And morning really is best, so make the effort: if a morning zombie like me can do it, you have no excuse whatsoever.) Find a quiet room where you won't be disturbed, and a comfortable chair.

Begin by thinking about your feet. Curl your toes away from your body. This creates muscular tension in your feet (and the tendons of your ankle for good measure.) Hold this tension as tight as you can manage and *think* about the way the tension feels. Pay attention to what's happening to your feet. Hold the toes curled tight a little longer, then let go. Let your feet relax. Let all the tension go. And *think about the feeling of relaxation in your feet*. Think about the difference between the feeling of tension a moment ago and the present feeling of relaxation.

Next, curl your feet in the opposite direction, as if your toes were trying to point towards your head. This creates tension in the calf muscles of your lower legs. Think about that feeling of tension, pay attention to the feel of your tight calf muscles . . . then let the tension go and think about the difference between the earlier tension and the present relaxation.

Now turn your attention to your thigh muscles. Tighten them up, hold them tight, tense and uncomfortable; think about the feeling of tension . . . then let go and think about the feeling of relaxation.

Beginning to get the idea?

You're sitting on the next group of muscles you'll be working on. Your bottom, in fact, is comprised of the largest muscle in the whole human body—and it does get tense, just like other muscle groups. Tighten it up, hold it tight, think about the sensation of the tension, then let go and think about the way it feels now you've relaxed.

Move on to your stomach and abdomen and repeat the process. Do the same with your shoulders, hunching them up around your ears to tighten the muscles, thinking about the tension, then letting go and thinking about the relaxation.

Next, do the trick with your arms, then your hands. Next, tighten up the multitude of little muscles in your face by gritting your teeth and grimacing. (You can see now why it's best to make sure you aren't disturbed.) Think about the tension in your face and jaw, hold the muscles tight, then let go and think about the relaxation. Finally, you should frown and raise your eyebrows to tighten the muscles of your scalp. Once again, think about the tension. Once again, let go and think about the difference between the tension and the relaxation.

By now you should be fairly well relaxed. The systematic tensing and relaxing of specific muscle groups works wonders at unknotting the worst of our unconscious tensions. You may find, however, particularly in the early days, that when you cast your mind over those muscle groups in the same sequence as before, new tensions have crept in here and there. If so, tighten the muscle group further, think about the tension, then let go and think for a moment about the relaxation. Finally, take a deep breath and sigh aloud.

That's it: the whole exercise for Week 1. Do it at least once at the same time each morning for the whole seven-day week. Then move on to Week 2.

Week 2

If you have faithfully carried out your relaxation exercise daily for the past week, you should be feeling at least a little benefit by now. I won't pretend you'll be any more relaxed generally, but you should be relaxing more quickly and easily during your morning session; and afterwards, you should be feeling considerably refreshed. There is a small but definite chance that you may feel more energetic throughout your day. None of this will be any big deal, but there should be just enough of a chance to encourage you to keep on.

This is, in fact, what you will be doing during Week 2. Same time each morning. Same quiet room. Same relaxation sequence as Week 1 . . . but with something important added.

Here comes the Pavlovian bit. When you reach the end of your standard exercise—the part where you take a deep breath and sigh aloud—I want you to repeat the word *green* while thinking about the colour green. Repeat the word aloud immediately following the sigh. Just once will do, but don't forget, because you are now into one of the most important parts of the whole exercise.

When you sigh aloud—the more explosively the better—the body responds by letting go of tension that little bit more. By speaking the word *green* and thinking of the colour green each time you reach your most relaxed state after the sequential tensing and relaxing of your muscles, you will in time begin to *associate* the colour green with relaxation. In Pavlovian terms, you are *conditioning yourself* to react with relaxation in association with the colour green. (Psychologists will in any case tell you that green is a restful colour, a fact which makes it particularly suitable for such an association.)

Since people will often expect miracles, you should know that your self-conditioning will not be complete in a week, or two weeks, or even three. But provided you practise daily, provided you speak the word *green* aloud and think green each time you reach that exceptionally relaxed state after your final sigh, then you can confidently expect that after *ten weeks* you will have a firm psychological linkage between green and relaxation.

Week 3

Continue your relaxation exercise exactly as for Week 2, including the sigh at the end and the enunciation of the word *green*. But this week, you might like to strengthen the green/relaxation linkage by wearing something green or ensuring you have something green to look at when the appropriate time arrives.

A word about the *shade* of green might not go amiss. There is nothing particularly restful about a dazzling lime green. So when you select green or think green, make it a grass green or a slightly darker leaf green. This choice of natural organic shades is not arbitrary: Nature has conditioned us for most of our lives and it makes sense to take advantage of this wherever possible.

Week 4

By now you should be getting pretty proficient in relaxation—and probably pretty bored with the whole tense-relax sequence. But I want you to stick it out just for one more week to make sure you really know all there is to know about the way tension feels in various muscle groups. There are, however, a couple of minor changes which may help a little with the tedium.

The first is that you can now experiment with the overall sequence, by trying to sense other muscle groups which you can then tense and relax. Your body is a complex machine and learning more about its remarkable muscular interactions will bring you nothing but benefit. The discovery of separate and distinct muscle groupings which you can work on consciously will also help increase your final level of relaxation.

The second is that you can now begin to *internalize* your self-conditioning. It's all very well conditioning yourself to relax when you say the word *green*, but if you have to keep chanting *green* in public every time you get a little tense, they are likely to cart you off to the Funny Farm! The trick is therefore to develop a conditioned reflex which comes into play when you *mentally* repeat the word. So from now on, every time you say *green* aloud after your relaxation exercise, be sure to pronounce it one more time *mentally* as well.

Week 5

After four weeks of daily relaxation practice, you should be something of an expert in the subject by now. In fact, you may have reached the stage where you don't have to go through that whole tense-relax routine anymore.

On the first day of Week 5, I want you to try it out. Instead of going through the routine as before, simply sit down, sigh, repeat the word *green* and relax totally.

This is something that either you can do or you can't; and the only one who can judge that is you. Certainly you will be able to relax to some degree. The question is whether you can relax as effectively as you could when you went through the whole sequence.

If you find you *can't*, then simply return to that original sequence for another week . . . or two weeks . . . or four weeks . . . or as long as it takes.

If, however, you find you can, things get easier. First of all, replace your morning exercise with twenty minutes morning relaxation. Go to your quiet room, sit in your comfortable chair, sigh, say *green* and let go of your tensions. Then simply stay relaxed for twenty minutes.

This is actually a lot more tricky than it sounds. Most tensions are the result of a lifetime habit and lifetime habits are difficult to break. Although you will almost certainly be able to relax very well for a short time, the chances are that new tensions will begin to creep in after a minute or two. Throughout this fifth week, it's your job to watch out for them, to spot new tensions are they arise; and to let them go. Keep this up until you are really proficient; until, that is, you sense tension and release it automatically. You may manage this within the week; if not, keep going until you do.

At this stage of your development as a wholly relaxed

individual, you might like to add in a few catch exercises to speed up your overall progress. At any suitable time throughout the day, simply think *green* and let go of your tensions.

Week 6 to Week 12

You're now halfway through your course and in case you haven't noticed, not once have you done anything about sending out Midas signals. Don't let this worry you. You have been preparing the way for everything that comes next, making sure your efforts will be as effective as possible.

I've already touched on the rationale behind the next phase of your course: you are enlisting the aid of your own unconscious mind by relaxing sufficiently to lower the barrier between it and your conscious self.

Another way of looking at it is to study what happens during hypnosis. When a subject goes into trance, suggestions made by the hypnotist are readily accepted, however bizarre those suggestions might be. Thus, if the hypnotist suggests that the subject has temporarily changed into a dog, then the subject will bark: something we must assume he would be unlikely to do in his normal waking state.

Deep relaxation has certain of the hallmarks of the hypnotic state. Among them is the fact that, when relaxed, you are more susceptible to suggestion. Since you have now spent five weeks learning how to deepen your level of relaxation, it is time you began to give yourself suggestions.

Emile Coué, the father of auto-suggestion, taught his followers to tell themselves repeatedly, 'Every day and in every way I am getting better and better.' While the system produced undoubted therapeutic results, later practitioners discovered a better way. That way was pictorial suggestions.

Coué's approach was verbal. He used words to carry the message. But there is a body of evidence pointing to the fact that the unconcious mind does not think in words, but rather in *pictures*. Thus pictorial suggestions have a greater chance of achieving results. But pictorial suggestions are not simply mental mock-ups. Correctly done, they involve a *total* act of your imagination.

For the remainder of your course, devote your morning session to the following procedure:

1. Trigger deep relaxation with the sigh and mental pronunciation of the word *green*.
2. Ensure no new tension creeps back in.
3. Close your eyes and imagine what it would be like to be rich.

Stage 3 is, of course, the vital one and involves a lot more than a woolly daydream. Start off by imagining yourself in a typical situation: a believable, day-to-day situation. The difference is that you are now rich.

Avoid any cartoon nonsense about lighting your cigar with £100 notes. The key to what you are doing is absolute realism. Imagine first how you would look. Better-quality clothes certainly—but what style of clothes? Would you go for a Savile Row suit or something less formal? Would you dress for comfort of fashion? Would you be extremely neat or ostentatiously scruffy?

How would you look, apart from your clothes? How would your hair be styled? What sort of shoes would you be wearing? What make and type of wrist-watch would you have? Would you go in for diamond tie-pins or personal jewellery? Do you prefer gold to silver? Would your nails be manicured? Would your skin be tanned from your last holiday in Bermuda? Would your image include dark glasses?

Once you have decided how you would look, try to imagine how you would feel. Be sensible and subtle. Becoming rich is *not* the same as being perpetually drunk: you will not feel high all the time. But you may well feel more confident; and you should certainly feel more relaxed about money. This is an area which is absolutely personal and one which will repay careful consideration. The question is not how one would feel if one were rich, but how *you* would feel if you were rich. Take as much time as you need to decide, then try to imagine the feeling.

Once you have determined how you would feel, try to imagine how you would *act*. This is not developed in isolation: it arises naturally out of how you would feel.

What you are doing here is creating an imaginary scenario with yourself as the central player. You need to do it as vividly and with as much detail as you can manage, so that in your relaxed state you almost feel yourself *living* the scenario.

Do this on a daily basis for the remainder of your course, varying the mental scenarios as often as you need in order to avoid boredom. And over the weeks you will find subtle changes occurring in yourself as your unconcious begins to accept the suggestions you are giving it.

These changes, in themselves, will sooner or later begin to have an impact on how people treat you, for they are changes which underpin the signals you send out. What you are doing here is smoothing your personal road to riches. But developing the Midas Signals is only one small part of the process. Alongside them you will also have to develop the Money Mentality, without which your exercises in imagination will remain only dreams.

5
THE CORNFELD
DILEMMA

In the Jewish community, one of the highest compliments you can be paid is to be called a *mench*. A mench is an all-round good guy; somebody who is pleasant to be with and who does the right and decent thing as if by instinct. But like many Yiddish words, this one is difficult to translate with absolute precision. Consequently it is sometimes defined by means of a story.

As this story is told, you are asked to imagine that while you are sitting in your office one wet Monday, the Devil appears with a black box under one arm. On the top of the black box is a large red button. At the side is a slot similar to those found in the automated tellers outside most modern banks.

The Devil makes a little small talk about how long it is since he's seen you, then presents you with the box, which you are unable to refuse. He tells you that, like all gifts from the Devil, it is impossible to return or throw away: the box will be with you to the end of your life.

(The good news is that he mentions the end of your life is very far away. According to his last astrological calculation, you will live far beyond the Biblical three-score years and ten; and remain healthy, fit and active into the bargain.)

The box, says the Devil, is an ingenious device based, like almost everything else nowadays, on microchip technology. It is a money-making machine. Every time you press the button on the top, there will emerge from the side slot, after a three-minute pause, a packet of crisp new banknotes to a total value of £1,000 sterling.

The Devil emphasizes that these are quite genuine banknotes. There are no forgeries amongst them and they are all legally acquired, actually forming a small part of the Devil's own income derived from a portfolio of shrewd investments built up over several thousand years.

There is no penalty to you for pressing the button, which you may, in fact, do as often as you wish. You will not lose your soul or anything of that nature since the Devil now has more souls than he needs and is actually facing a slight accommodation problem in Hell.

There is, however, one small drawback associated with the use of the box: every time you press the button, a peasant dies in China.

The Devil is quick to reassure you about how small a problem this actually represents. More than a quarter of the world's population is concentrated in China. Statistically, a peasant dies every three minutes anyway, so that even if you were to press the button non-stop for the remainder of your life, you would make no real difference to the overall number of deaths. Furthermore, he is perfectly prepared to sign a cast-iron copper-bottomed guarantee in blood that those who die will never be friends or relatives of yours; you will never know them personally or have contact with them, their friends or families, in any way. That, as the Devil disappears in the traditional cloud of sulphurous smoke, is the deal.

The point of this story arrives when you learn that a mench is defined as somebody who would never press the button. The reason for repeating it here is to ask how often you think *you* would press that button.

The Cornfeld Dilemma

Robert Hayes-McCoy, a man interested in what makes people tick, once asked me how I would spend a million pounds if he gave it to me in a paper parcel, no strings attached. I thought for a while, then told him, but he had already lost interest.

'You took seventeen seconds to answer,' he told me. 'Anybody who really *wanted* a million would know what he was going to do with it right away. You didn't. You'd *like* a million, but you don't really *want* it.'

The insight is interesting and highlights something you are going to have to tackle on your road to fortune: the Cornfeld Dilemma.

Bernie Cornfeld, a man destined to end suffering for his part in certain convoluted practices involving high finance, used to ask potential investors a highly charged question:

'Do you *sincerely* want to be rich?'

If the question were put to you, as the question about the million pounds was put to me, how would you answer? And before you say a word, it might be useful to discuss a little theory here.

Howard Hughes, one of the richest men who ever lived, made his fortune in aircraft and the movie industry. (He was the model for the central character in Harold Robbins' best-selling novel *The Carpetbaggers*.) Hughes became rich when he was still young enough—so one might imagine—to enjoy it. But he ended his life a total recluse, terrified to meet people or even touch a doorknob lest he pick up germs.

The late J. Paul Getty, a self-made oil multi-millionaire, was reputed in later life to be a very lonely man, living as a virtual prisoner in a mansion surrounded by security systems and guard dogs.

One must, of course, be careful here. There are a great many lonely paupers and if Getty was miserable, he was at least miserable in comfort. Hughes, in turn, suffered from a psychiatric condition which was neither caused by money nor confined to the rich.

Nevertheless, there is more than a grain of truth in the old saw that money can't buy happiness, although most of our social programmes and almost all political economics is based on the assumption that it can. Yet the Scandinavian countries manage to combine one of the world's highest living standards with one of the world's highest suicide rates. Scandinavian wealth may not *cause* unhappiness, but it certainly does not prevent it.

There are, however, certain absolute drawbacks to the possession of great wealth. Most of them may be loosely grouped under the generic heading of Security.

A few years ago, watching a news broadcast from a millionaire's convention, I discovered that each of the delegates had been issued with a personal firearm for his own protection. General security was, of course, extremely tight, but the organizers felt this last line of defence necessary because of the high risk of kidnapping for ransom. A small selection of the millionaires were interviewed in the course of the broadcast. None of them looked particularly relaxed. (Although it dilutes the point I am making, I feel compelled to mention that one Indian delegate retained his sense of humour and refused to carry a gun or take any special security precautions. When questioned about this, he said he could not imagine any kidnapper mad enough to want a ransom in rupees!)

The psychology of money is most peculiar. C. Northcliff Parkinson shot to fame when he reported the 'commonplace observation' that all work expands to fill the time available for its completion. The desire for money is a little like that. Somehow what you have is never quite enough to purchase the feeling of security you need. When you are fighting a bank overdraft, you imagine that a credit balance of £1,000 would leave you feeling happy and relaxed. Once you achieve this credit balance, however, you move your own mental goalposts and decide that really only £5,000 would purchase the well-being you desire. At £5,000 the goal becomes £10,000 or £20,000 or more. You are walking towards a receding horizon: a reason why so many extremely wealthy people continue to work hard to earn more money than they could possibly ever spend.

Once great wealth is achieved, it is a personal observation

that a sense of worth or well-being does not automatically follow. Furthermore, wealth creates its own peculiar insecurities, as the conference delegates must have long since discovered. If you are flat broke, you may have many problems, but the fear of being robbed or swindled is not one of them. Security becomes a major preoccupation of the very rich: and security defined in its broadest sense. Once you have money, it is human to want to keep it. Even without thieves and swindlers, this is not always easy to do.

The Rule of 72

In an earlier chapter, we have discussed the magic of compound interest. The Rule of 72 makes it more magic still.

The Rule of 72 is a simple but very useful little calculation. If you divide 72 by the annual percentage interest paid on a deposit, your answer gives you a rough indication of how long it will be before compound interest doubles your money.

But doubling your money is a big deal only in periods of no, or low, inflation. When inflation is high—and a study of economic history over the past 200 years suggests inflationary spirals are as inevitable as wars and may actually arise on a cyclical basis—it is far more difficult to double your money in real terms, whatever the Rule of 72 may suggest. When inflation really runs riot (as it did, for example, from the middle 1960s through to the early 1970s) the problem is not how to double your money, but how to maintain the spending power of the money you already have. At times like this, a simple bank deposit is seldom enough: cash in the vaults rots away faster than the interest top-up can replace it.

In circumstances like these, the very rich develop problems. They may be high-class problems, but they are problems none the less. Maintaining levels becomes a major preoccupation. The discovery is made that having money is a bit like having children. Both seem fine in theory, but once they come along, they need a lot of looking after.

The Money Mentality

The problems of having money are not the only reason why you should squarely face the Cornfeld Dilemma. Another reason is the sort of person you must be to get it.

A. E. van Vogt is perhaps best known as a science fiction writer. In 1972, however, he published a book that fell a long way from this category. It was called *The Money Personality*. This book was the distillation of a lifetime's observation of rich people. In it, van Vogt explained that such people exhibited twelve—and only twelve—special personality characteristics related to their wealth.

I am not sure I agree with van Vogt that the characteristics are limited to twelve. Nor would I accept that every wealthy person need necessarily have all traits listed. But my own experience confirms many of his insights.

A. E. van Vogt listed the twelve qualities in synopsis as follows:

1. In all commercial transactions, the money personality refuses to be a victim, requiring valid agreements in writing and fulfilment of contracts.

2. The money personality sets himself, or accepts from others, assignments that are specific and that he knows he can carry out.

3. The money personality always has a personal, special reason for charging a profit.

4. The money personality stays awake and alert all day long, preferably with suitable exercise.

5. The money personality understands human nature sufficiently so that he invariably includes that understanding in any deal and wants to know where the money will come from and when.

6. The money personality competes for real rewards, either as a member of a group or as an individual.

7. The high social IQ necessary for the money personality is acquirable in four clearcut steps.

8. The money personality has a special, intense, meaningful interest in his work and thereby creates wealth that never existed before.

9. The money personality is a giver of gifts as an automatic defence against the immature desire to be taken care of.

10. The money personality recognizes signals of success or failure and at once acts accordingly.

11. The money personality trains himself in a few key winning habits.

12. The money personality orients to money or to a winner.

There are a lot of important insights in that list and we may well be returning to a few of them later. But for the moment, take it one step at a time, accept that these are genuine money-oriented characteristics and ask yourself if that's *really* the sort of person you want to be.

1. In all commercial transactions, the money personality refuses to be a victim, requiring valid agreements in writing and fulfilment of contracts.

A. E. van Vogt discovered that a large body of people (mainly male) are *victims*. They put up with shoddy workmanship and minor swindles because they don't like to make a fuss. They walk away rather than fight for their rights.

Unfortunately the term 'victim' is emotive. Of course you don't want to be a victim; and that presumes you want to be the opposite. Or does it? Are you *really* the sort of person who wants to put everything in writing? Are you *really* the sort of person who wants to make a fuss every time the service you're paying for falls a little short? I have two business colleagues who carefully add up the bill each time it is presented and scream at the waiter if there is the slightest discrepancy. They never get ripped off; but most of the time they dine alone. Maybe there really are instances when being a victim isn't so bad. Maybe you'd rather be liked than rich.

2. The money personality sets himself, or accepts from others, assignments that are specific and that he knows he can carry out.

So you set yourself assignments or accept assignments you

know you can carry out. That's great. I live in a country where just about anybody will accept an assignment knowing full well there isn't a snowball's chance in hell that he can carry it out. People do this because they don't like to say 'No' and disappoint you. The fact that you'll still be disappointed when they don't deliver hardly matters: it's a long way down the road.

So the assignment characteristic looks pretty okay. And certainly if you accept assignments and manage to deliver every time, you'll do well *and* gain a whole heap of popularity. But doesn't that bit about *giving yourself* assignments ring a few small warning bells? Doesn't it have just the hint of an all work and no play situation?

It is, of course, true to say that some rich people are extremely idle. But people who are in the process of *getting* rich seldom fall into this category. For most of them it's work, work, work—which may be why so many career executives suffer from bad or broken marriages, estranged children, ulcers and high blood pressure. Maybe you can cope with the pressure better than most (and the relaxation reflex you built up in the last chapter will certainly help) but do you really want an all-work lifestyle? According to van Vogt, if you want to get rich, it comes with the territory.

3. The money personality always has a personal, special reason for charging a profit.

When you read the chapter in van Vogt's book that deals with this characteristic, you quickly discover that the reasons people gave him as justification for taking a profit were often invalid. Furthermore, van Vogt comes right out in the open and tells you that this doesn't matter. So long as *you* are satisfied with the reason, the characteristic still works to make you money.

So now you need to ask yourself if you really want to be rich at the price of continual self deception?

4. The money personality stays awake and alert all day long, preferably with suitable exercise.

Since I got to be middle-aged, I have become a great believer in exercise. This belief has even withstood those upsetting newspaper reports of people who drop dead from heart attacks while jogging. And there is something fine about staying awake and alert all day. You might say that the inner dynamo is something you have to be born with, not something you can actually develop; and I might agree with you. But I imagine you're like most people and would enjoy very much being fit, alert, healthy and active.

If, however, you are not fit, alert, healthy and active right now, you might pause a moment and ask yourself why. It might be illness, of course, and if so that's all right. But if you're like most of us, you're that way because you don't want to make the effort to exercise. I can tell you right now that if you won't make the effort for the sake of a healthy body, you certainly aren't going to make it for the sake of getting rich.

5. *The money personality understands human nature sufficiently so that he invariably includes that understanding in any deal and wants to know where the money will come from and when.*

There is a hint of cynicism in the wording of this one that belies the actuality, which is concerned specifically with business enterprises. What van Vogt is saying is that business is about making money not about indulging your fantasies of how the world should be.

While I would tend to agree with this overall and certainly agree that the attitude is a road to riches, the point at issue here is whether you really want to be the sort of person who operates a business only for money. The profit motive is a major reason why people go into business; perhaps *the* major reason. But it certainly is not the *only* reason. You might, for example, go into a particular line of business because you wished to be of service to the community. Or you might want to cover the costs of doing something you enjoy. These may be minority reasons for going into business, but they remain valid ones. I write for a living and sell what I write. But if no one bought my output, I would continue to write anyway: for me it is less a business than an itch which needs constant scratching. The question here is does money turn you on so much that you will never work for enjoyment?

6. *The money personality competes for real rewards, either as a member of a group or as an individual.*

Real rewards? For the money personality, real rewards are defined as money. Perhaps you would define them differently?

7. *The high social IQ necessary for the money personality is acquirable in four clearcut steps.*

However a high social IQ is achieved, it is worth looking at what van Vogt meant by a high social IQ in the first place. It transpires that what he means is popularity: specifically, popularity combined with the common touch.

In marketing, any vendor with the common touch is worth his weight in gold since he knows instinctively what product to offer, what price level to select and what sort of promotional strategy to adopt. So once again van Vogt seems to be right in suggesting a personality trait which attracts money.

One wonders, however, whether the common touch is all it's made out to be in personal terms. Most of us envy popular people; yet those same popular people are under constant pressure. They are seldom alone. They rarely find time, in the poet's words to stand and stare. Is this what you want?

8. *The money personality has a special, intense, meaningful interest in his work and thereby creates wealth that never existed before.*

There is no doubt at all that an intense, meaningful interest in work is a very satisfying thing to develop. But it has at least two drawbacks.

The first is that it tends to make work an addiction. One sees the results in top executives everywhere. Their work comes before home, before marriage, before children. They bemoan a God who saw fit to put only twenty-four hours in a day. Their lives are their jobs and outside the work context they are often crashing bores since, like all addicts, they have tightly confined, single-track minds.

The second drawback is the situation which arises when work stops: during a recession, for example, or, with greater inevitability, on retirement.

The notorious Wall Street Crash stimulated so many suicides that one seldom stops to consider how odd a response suicide is to corporate loss. Are work and money really so important that their (usually temporary) withdrawal is worth your very life?

If the example seems a little remote, consider a far more commonplace example of the deadly results of work addiction. If you have friends in business, it is a racing certainty that you know, or have heard of, at least one case where a man retires fit and healthy at sixty or sixty-five and is dead within two years. The syndrome is so commonplace it is now the subject of social and medical studies. But even the experts agree about the cause: the dear departed was addicted to his work and could not live without his fix.

9. The money personality is a giver of gifts as an automatic defence against the immature desire to be taken care of.

Most of us would agree that to be a giver of gifts is a laudable thing. But van Vogt leaps into a curious abyss when he describes the desire to be taken care of as 'immature'.

Almost all of us exhibit a need to be taken care of at some time or another: it is what many of the world's major religions are all about. Arguably, we deny such needs at our peril and no amount of pejorative labelling is going to protect us.

10. The money personality recognizes signals of success or failure and acts at once accordingly.

This one seems free and clear of any drawbacks until you read van Vogt's full explanation. Then you realize that alertness to signals can be a royal road to constant worry as well as to riches. Not all signals are pleasant; and the least pleasant are often the most important. Nobody admires the ostrich, but sometimes a well-buried head is the only thing that will preserve your sanity.

11. The money personality trains himself in a few key winning habits.

It is interesting to discover what van Vogt considers to be winning habits from his study of the rich. Among them he lists daily exercise, punctuality, social graces and elegant language. Among losing habits are things like boasting and vulgarity.

All of us claim to be for good and against evil, so it is easy to agree that boasting and vulgarity are things to be avoided . . . except that most of us like to indulge in just a little of each now and then. If we are not careful, our pursuit of money may put us in a very uncomfortable strait-jacket.

12. The money personality orients to money or to a winner.

This is, perhaps, the most crucial trait of all; and the one on which I most readily agree with van Vogt. If there is one characteristic which marks out money-makers, it is their bedrock obsession with making money. It comes ahead of friendship, comfort, love and many other desirable things and leads us to pose once again that single-question quiz which absolutely determines whether you are destined for wealth: Do you sincerely want to be rich?

Once you start to think about it, the answer isn't all that obvious, because getting rich and being rich don't seem to be quite the fun things you imagined. But if you don't (sincerely) want to be rich, no amount of books like this one will help you make it. You will read with interest and fail to apply the lessons outlined.

If, on consideration, you discover you do not now really want to pay the price of riches, pass this book on to a friend. What comes next is not for you.

6
MANUFACTURING THE MONEY MENTALITY

It isn't *quite* true to say that nobody ever got rich working for other people. But it's close.

There are executives whose annual earnings top the £ million mark, but not many. More to the point, what they earn (however large) is always less than the wealth they create, otherwise it would make no sense to employ them. They may be rich, but their boss is always richer.

There is nothing wrong with this situation. When you enter employment, you sell your particular skills and talents for more than money. Intangibles like security, regularity of income, freedom from certain worries, all form part of the unspoken contract. For many people—indeed for most people—the deal is a good one. But if you have solved the Cornfeld Dilemma and sincerely want to get rich, then you can forget about working for somebody else. Your chances of making it big take a quantum leap once you decide to work for yourself.

There are several ways of doing so, none of them easy. You might, for example, elect to follow a profession, given that your qualifications are in order. Many doctors are self-employed, as are many architects and accountants. Most achieve comfortable incomes, but it is probably true to say that few are really rich. The exceptions are usually found in *partnerships*, professional collectives in which mutual support and a spread of service tends to generate additional wealth.

Another form of self-employment is *freelancing*, an approach which tends to be favoured by those with a specific talent: writers, designers, artists and so on. People of this sort often begin their careers in employment, but decide eventually that they might be better off selling their talents piecemeal on the open market. Income levels within this group tend to vary far more widely than among professionals; but like professionals, it is probably fair to say only a minority of freelances become wealthy.

A third self-employment grouping is in many ways the most interesting, since it holds promise of the greatest rewards and is not confined to people with specific qualifications or talents. This is the *business* grouping; and you can join it with no more effort than the decision to become an entrepreneur.

Not all entrepreneurs get rich, of course, but the possibility of real wealth is somewhat higher in this grouping than in the professional or freelance counterparts. Furthermore—and this is probably the most important insight into the entrepreneural group—the skills and instincts developed by the successful entrepreneur may be applied within the other groupings to achieve substantial financial rewards.

Though simple, this is not a particularly easy concept to grasp, but two contrasting illustrations will make the point.

The best medical practitioner I have ever met is a South African working in private practice in Europe. Her diagnostic and therapeutic skills are remarkable by any criteria. Since she favours unorthodox medical techniques, the bulk of her practice is made up of patients abandoned as incurable by other doctors. Despite this, her success rate is far greater than the average. Her reputation stands extremely high in the country where she works. She is consulted by politicians and celebrities.

You might imagine from all this that we are discussing a very wealthy woman. In fact, it would be no exaggeration to describe her as poor. At any given time over the past three years, it has been touch and go whether her practice would continue or slide quietly into bankruptcy.

The contrasting case is an artist colleague of mine; a man with much graphic talent, an appetite for work and a creative obsession. In his early years, he supported himself as a designer within the advertising industry. More recently, he has turned increasingly to the paintings of pictures as his major outlet.

For those with any knowledge of the field, this development must seem like a recipe for financial disaster. The great artist starving in a garret has become a cliché. This great artist is not, however, starving. On the contrary, he is currently on the way to considerable wealth.

What is the essential difference between these two people? Not talent, certainly. The South African doctor is as talented in her own field as the artist is in his. Not the excellence of their service either. Both do the very best they can to provide the very best 'product' they are able.

Nor is there any difference in the effort they put into their work. Both are open for business at least six days a week; often seven. Both work long hours. And while we are not, of course, comparing like with like, it is difficult to argue that there is a perceived difference in the final value of what they do: art and health are both seen as highly desirable commodities in our culture.

The huge difference between the two is *commercial instinct*. The artist has it in abundance, the doctor not at all. The artist is, in fact, an entrepreneur who searches endlessly for ways to exploit his own considerable talent. He publishes, distributes and markets books and portfolios of his own art. He broadcasts and lectures frequently. He has a public relations consultant on permanent retainer.

A doctor cannot, of course, go the same route as the artist. Medical ethics preclude overt self-advertisement. But medical ethics do not preclude image-building and good business sense. The practitioner we are discussing charges minimal fees in order to assist as many patients as possible. She will also extend credit to anyone who asks, thus guaranteeing that in many cases even the minimal fees are never paid. Wealthy patients are treated no differently from any others, so that she does not even attempt the Robin Hood approach of robbing the rich to pay for the poor. Her surgery is drab. She acts as her own receptionist and practises in a poor quarter of town. What she does is praiseworthy by any standard, but she will never attract money.

The Selling Secret

Van Vogt's personality attributes aside, there is one realization central to manufacturing the money mentality. It is a secret applied by everyone who makes money, whether they realize it or not. It is a secret I have revealed in articles and lectures and while it is almost unbelievably simple, it always comes as a surprise to those who receive it. The secret it this:

Learn to sell and you'll get rich!

There is, however, a secret within a secret here; and the secret within the secret is how you define the word 'sell'. Because what will make you rich isn't selling brushes door to door, isn't selling cars from a plush showroom, isn't selling a product at all, in fact. What will make you rich is *selling yourself*.

We'll be coming back to this in the next chapter. In the interim, you need to pay attention to something a lot less exciting but even more important: your *first step* on the road to riches.

First Step to Wealth

You'd imagine your first step to wealth would be a real buzz, but it isn't. It is, in fact, almost unbelievably dull and boring. You will find it seems to contradict something I told you earlier; and it certainly looks like a pretty straightforward way of going nowhere. To give it to you right between the eyes, your first step on the road to riches is to get yourself a job.

So almost nobody gets rich working for other people and yet I want you to go right out there and start working for somebody else? Too right I do, and here's the reason why.

Sooner or later you are going to start working for yourself. Now you've decided you sincerely want to get rich, that is quite inevitable. To work for yourself successfully you will need experience, business skills, energy, luck and, above all, money.

Starting a business is easy: you hang out your sign. Making a profit is easy: you buy at a penny and sell for tuppence. Staying in business is a lot more difficult. And contrary to what you may believe, most bankrupt businesses fail not because of losses, but because of cash flow or under-capitalization (frequently two symptoms of the same disease).

Business is a golden poker game and to get in on the action you need a stake. Some, perhaps most, of that stake will be borrowed. But some will—and should—be your own money.

So when I suggest you find yourself a job, it is important to remember that the job is just a stepping stone. It should never be seen as a career in its own right, but rather as a means of creating the stake you need to get into business in your own right.

Once you start thinking like this (and it's a way of thinking that is part of the money mentality) you will find there is really only one criterion for the sort of job you select: how much money will it allow you to save?

Note that word *save*. A job which allows you to *make* a great deal of money is not necessarily the same thing as a job which allows you to *save* a great deal of money. Many highly paid jobs generate their own expenses. They call on you to dress well and maintain a certain lifestyle. You live enjoyably enough, but your ability to accumulate capital is virtually zero. What you are looking for is employment which generates no such expenses and ideally takes care of such expenses as you may already have. Employment which feeds and houses you is by no means confined to top management. Roughnecks working on an oil rig are routinely housed and fed during their stint offshore. They are also clothed, since the prevailing conditions require it. Nor is the oil industry the only area of employment in which you can routinely enjoy such perks. I know one man who is chauffeured by his clients to every job he does, housed, fed and entertained for the duration of his work then driven home gratefully when the job is completed. He is a thatcher and the money he earns is largely a capital accumulation.

How To Get a Job

Finding a job is up to you: even in this age of high unemployment, the Situations Vacant columns are full of them. Actually *getting* a job is usually more tricky, so you may appreciate a litle help.

Getting an Interview

In most worthwhile jobs, your first hurdle is to ensure that you join the list of applicants who are favoured with an interview. For many, the hurdle seems enormous, yet getting an interview is extremely easy once you know how. In another of my books, I told the story of a colleague who was once a *professional* interviewee. He would seek out posts which offered to pay expenses should an applicant be called for an interview. So easy did he find it to get to the interview stage that he actually managed to live off these expenses—and live so well that when jobs were offered, he routinely turned them down.

Your first step towards getting an interview is to find out what the prospective employer actually *wants*. This is not quite so easy as it sounds. Employers spend a great deal of money and effort advertising for staff and far too often manage to do so without saying plainly what it is they want.

Not so long ago I was called in to advise a large State organization on why its recruitment advertising attracted such low-calibre applicants. I analysed several of the ads then spoke to the committee which had created them. One required applicants to have 'communication skills'. I told the committee I did not understand what this phrase meant and asked for an explanation. The committee chairman assured me the phrase was well enough understood by the type of person they wanted to attract. I pressed for an explanation none the less. A committee member gave me a definition—which was promptly contradicted by two other members and the chairman. I stopped the ensuing argument after five minutes: long enough to demonstrate that those who drew up the ad did not know what communication skills meant—or rather, they defined the term differently from one another. And if the employer who creates the ad does not know what is meant, the potential applicant has a very poor chance indeed.

Poor chance or not, you are going to have to make the effort. Don't just read the ad (and certainly don't just take what it says at face value.) Try instead to put yourself in the employer's place. Try to imagine the employer's problems and figure out what sort of employee would solve them. Be creative: sometimes the most important criteria never appear in the ad at all.

> ### VAN SALESPERSON
> ### WANTED
> **Clean Driving Licence essential**

That little ad was run by a bakery and in seven words illustrates just about everything I've been saying about how badly some employers communicate their needs. A driving licence is certainly essential if you are going to take a job as a van salesperson. But a *clean* driving licence? The fact that you have, say, one endorsement does not make you a lunatic on the road. But this particular bakery had a bad experience of a driver who was indeed a lunatic on the road and sent their insurance premiums sky high by smashing up two vans within a week. Thus the company was extremely sensitive about the question of clean driving licences.

None the less, whatever the bakery management thought they wanted, what they actually wanted was somebody who could do the job well. And a little thought would tell you this meant someone who had sales ability, a pleasing personality, good appearance and (since we are dealing with a food product) an appreciation of the value of hygiene. Experience in a similar sort of job might be useful. Good health would be an asset. And since bread vans deliver early, so too would high morning energy levels.

None of these requirements appeared in the original ad, but all of them might be deduced without too much difficulty by putting yourself in the employer's place. Exactly the same technique can be applied with equal success to advertisements for nuclear physicists or computer programmers. Once you take the trouble to put yourself in the employer's place and use your imagination, the precise needs of a given job are usually fairly obvious.

Your next step is your letter of application. If you are serious about the job this letter should be seen as an investment. If you are unable to type, find someone who will type it for you. If you are unable to spell, find someone who will *write* it for you. Beg, borrow or buy some good quality paper: you should actually only need one sheet since your letter of application will be short. Then sit down and think how you can make your letter stand out from the herd.

How To Create a Letter That Will GUARANTEE an Interview

It is a commonplace mistake to assume that the letter you write is a letter applying for the job. It is nothing of the sort. It is a letter applying for the *interview* and there is a world of difference.

Letters applying for jobs are (rightly) full of information about qualifications, background and experience. Letters applying for an interview are based on very different criteria.

An employer who offers you a job takes a very large step indeed. He or she is placing a large annual sum of money behind the decision in the form of salary and may be risking even more when one considers the damage you could do.

But the offer of an interview is different. Usually the only thing risked is a little time. Furthermore, an employer who advertises for staff is *strongly predisposed* to interview. Given that a candidate is neither drunk nor insane, there is no risk involved in granting the interview and a substantial risk in refusing. The employer, almost by definition, seeks the best person for the job. And where is the certainty that the best person has been found if even a few applicants are left uninterviewed?

Once you realize how anxious an employer is to interview you (while remaining hesitant to offer you the job), your letter of interview application becomes easy. There is, for example, no need to bore your reader with a lengthy document detailing your education, career background and qualifications. Leave that sort of nonsense to the herd. Your letter can be refreshingly short and to the point by following these simple guidelines.

Dear NAME . . .

If you don't know the name of the person you are writing to, find out. (A phone call to the company concerned will usually do the trick; and you will seldom have to go further than the switchboard operator. Explain why you want the name and you should get it without any problem.) Names are, of course, magic. At a crowded cocktail party your mind will screen out the background hum of conversation until your name is mentioned: then your attention is immediately grabbed. A letter beginning with the recipient's name gets off to a far better start than any of the multitude of 'Dear Sir/Madam'.

Your advertisement for a widget knocker in today's Evening Press
convinced me yours is the sort of company I'd like to work for . . .

Most letters of application begin with 'I'. Yours begins with
'You' (or rather 'Your'). The tone is immediately warmer and
the interest level of the reader automatically increases—
especially since what you go on to say suggests he has created
an excellent advertisement and is subtly flattering to his
company.

*I'm ideally suited to the post you advertise and would welcome an
opportunity of discussing my qualifications with you face to face.*

You'll note that you don't say what your qualifications are.
If you did there is a chance that the reader might not agree you
were indeed ideal. As it is, he has to talk to you to find out.
And why should he not do so? All he is risking is a little
interview time.

*Unless I hear from you to the contrary, I'll ring your secretary to
arrange a mutually suitable date and time* . . .

Now you've forced him to take action if he *doesn't* want to
see you and saved him the trouble of replying if he does. This
is a product-selling technique applied to an unusual situation.
It works for products and it will work for you. Overall, your
letter is quietly confident. It wastes little of your reader's time.
It intrigues. It presents what you want very clearly and it
makes it easier for the reader to deliver than refuse.

Above all, it is specially geared to getting you the interview,
not the job.

How to Convert the Interview

There is a story that the (male) managing director of a large
manufacturing company once called in a management
consultant to find him a private secretary.

The consultant advertised, screened a number of applicants,
then shortlisted three well-qualified young women for the final
interview. Having done so, he returned to the Chief Executive
and asked him to sit in on the interviews, but requested him to
say nothing until all three applicants had been vetted.

When the first woman entered the interview room, the consultant asked her a single question, 'What is two plus two?' She looked at him in surprise. 'Four, of course.' He thanked her and asked her to wait outside.

When the next applicant was given the same question, she looked at the consultant slyly. 'That's obviously a trick question,' she said. 'The answer can't be as simple as one would think, so I'll say it's twenty-two.' Again the consultant thanked her and dismissed her.

The third applicant thought for a moment when faced with the same question, then said, 'The arithmetical answer is obviously four, but there is a possibility that you are presenting the problem visually, joining two to two in sequence, in which the answer would undoubtedly be twenty-two.'

When this applicant left, the consultant turned to the managing director. 'Let us analyze the situation,' he said. 'The first applicant showed intelligence: she knew two and two was four. The second applicant showed imagination and initiative: she selected a much more unusual, but equally valid, answer of twenty-two. The third applicant, however, showed intelligence, imagination *and* initiative with her realization that there could actually be *two* answers, both equally valid in their own sets of circumstances. Now, sir, which applicant would you like to be your secretary?'

'I rather fancy the blonde in the tight sweater,' said the managing director.

The story illustrates not only the male chauvinism which is still unfortunately so rife in business, but also the fact that many—and possibly most—employers may be influenced by factors other than your immediate qualifications for the job. Tight sweaters apart, the most common factor of influence is personality.

So profound is this influence that I have frequently seen it outweigh actual qualifications in a competitive job-seeking situation. Applicants who are relaxed, calm, confident and downright *likeable* can often steal jobs from under the noses of their better-qualified but less personable rivals.

You are, of course, a warm and wonderful human being, but you may, in the past, have found a little difficulty in projecting these qualities strongly enough to influence others. The difficulty may have arisen through shyness, through nervousness, through inexperience or a hundred and one other factors. But it is there and it is something you will have to deal with, not only in a job-seeking situation, but in the entrepreneural career which you plan to follow your period of employment.

Fortunately all the information you need to do so is contained in our very next chapter.

7
CREATING A GOLDEN IMAGE

Image is an advertising term used to describe how a product is perceived by those who buy it. This perception is often unrelated to reality.

Not long ago I was called in to advise a major brick manufacturer which had run into quality control problems a few years earlier. As a result, a poor-quality product was produced and sales dropped alarmingly.

The company then invested substantially in a computerized production line, solved its quality problems and began once again to produce bricks of a high standard. But sales continued to fall.

The directors of the company were much more familiar with production than marketing and were at a loss to understand why they could no longer sell a quality product. I was able to tell them they were suffering from a problem of image.

During the period of production difficulties, potential purchasers had decided their bricks were poor quality. This perception became the image of the bricks in the marketplace. Now the bricks had changed, but the perception had not and sales continued to slump. No amount of product improvement will lift sales in competition with a negative image.

People can have image problems too. Film actors noted for tough roles frequently find men try to pick fights with them in bars: their screen image has overlaid their real life personality. Politicians—among them Margaret Thatcher and Ronald Reagan—have employed professionals to advise them on their image.

But the most interesting thing about image is that it can be *changed*. Coca-Cola started out as a medicinal tonic. It is now one of the world's most popular soft drinks. Jeans which started out as work clothes for the North American farmer, subsequently became the unofficial uniform of rebellious youth, and finally invaded the halls of high fashion. None of this could have happened without a change of image; indeed without a series of changes of image.

The Strength of Image

A few years ago, supermarkets began an interesting experiment. Faced with a shrinking consumer economy, they introduced onto their shelves a range of unbranded goods in plain, no-nonsense packaging, at substantial reductions in price over the more familiar branded item.

To reassure the buying public, it was announced that the low price did not reflect a loss of quality. Rather it was achieved by saving on advertising and packaging.

The goods concerned were popular staples—cornflakes, baked beans, bleach and the like—which were, indeed, of the highest quality since in many cases they were actually produced by the same companies which marketed the branded products. Often they were the *actual* branded product in plain wrapping.

When the concept was originally introduced there was an understandable hesitation by the brand manufacturers to go along with the scheme. It seemed obvious that if the housewife was faced with a choice between, say, a branded toothpaste at £1 and the same toothpaste, unbranded, for 80p she would not hesitate to buy the cheaper product.

But if the manufacturers feared they might be cutting their own throats, they were also squeezed by the purchasing power of the supermarkets and tempted by the bulk outlets the new scheme promised.

In practice, as it subsequently transpired, their fears

proved groundless. Branded and unbranded goods now co-exist quite happily in supermarkets. Shoppers cheerfully buy both.

This is quite a remarkable situation. Why should a sizeable percentage of shoppers ignore an inexpensive unbranded product in favour of the *same product* at a *higher price* in different packaging? The answer, simply, is image; and it is an answer which clearly demonstrates how strongly image can affect behaviour. Shoppers were—and are—prepared to pay extra for the reassurance of familiar brands and packaging with all their built-in image connotations.

Exactly the same phenomenon, writ large, is seen in the fact that some purchasers are prepared to pay almost as much for a car as they would for a house. Theoretically, a car is no more than a motorized box on wheels built to carry people from A to B. But try telling that to the man who has seen his first Rolls Royce or Porsche, brands unsurpassed in terms of image.

Manipulating an Image

In advertising, image manipulation is commonplace, sophisticated—and costly.

Many years ago, the Guinness Group undertook market research that indicated their main product—the world's most popular pint of stout—was favoured by a predominantly male market segment made up of older drinkers. And the image of the drink had shifted from the vaguely medicinal 'Guinness is Good for You' to something with more than a hint of an ageing macho.

These revelations were obviously bad news for the company. The discovery that you are selling to an ageing market is viewed by most executives as the kiss of death. Old markets die off and if you have not made some inroads into the next generation along, your product dies off with them.

In the case of Guinness, there was a second problem: the heavily masculine aspect of the image. This, by definition, diminished sales potential by some 50 per cent. A decision was made to change the image of the product.

That the decision was a good one I have no doubt. That it was a costly one I have no doubt either. For years now, Guinness advertising has presented a very clear-cut image of a younger generation drink favoured equally by men and women. Personality endorsements have been sought. Perhaps the most typical is that of Elkie Brookes: young, attractive, successful and, if we can believe the ads, a Guinness drinker.

Guinness are not, of course, the only company to engage in image manipulation. Compare any early motor car advertisement with the type of promotion that is commonplace today. The early advertising stressed utilitarian aspects. Today the emphasis is on style.

But if the major corporations are forced to spend thousands, often millions, on changing image, you will be pleased to learn that you are not. Once you cut through the mystique of image you will quickly find there is one central secret which you can press into service to enormous personal benefit. And that is the secret I propose to reveal to you right now.

The Chameleon Secret

Murray Raphel, a top US businessman and lecturer on marketing, tells the story of how his wife read an advertisement for her local bank and discovered they were running a special promotion to show how friendly they were.

According to the advertisement, if a customer did not get a smile and a friendly word from bank staff while conducting a transaction, the bank undertook to pay a dollar into that customer's account.

So the next time Ruth Raphel went into her bank, she waited in anticipation of the friendly word and smile. Neither came. The transaction was brisk, businesslike and totally distant. When it was completed, Mrs Raphel asked, 'Where's my dollar?'

The teller looked at her blankly.

'Where's my dollar?' Mrs Raphel repeated. 'I read an ad where it said you would pay me a dollar if you failed to smile and make a friendly remark.'

'That promotion was *last* week,' snapped the teller.

As a marketing adviser, I frequently meet with top executives who have strange ideas about the image of their companies.

Fairly typical was Mr B—, a marketing director of a major banking group, who told me in the course of a lengthy discussion that his bank was projecting a friendly image.

'Why do you say that?' I asked him.

'We have spent—' And here he named a figure only marginally short of the National Debt. '—on advertising and promotion, all of it geared towards projecting a friendly image. We have done market research into the memorability and recall of our advertising and the figures are batting more than 85 per cent.'

I told him that whatever the figures said, his bank was not projecting a friendly image. He asked me why I said so.

'I'm a customer of your bank,' I told him. 'I've been a customer for years. Your staff still don't know my name, what line of business I conduct or how well my wife is doing after her back operation. Your bank is businesslike and efficient, but friendly it is not.'

Mr B— was making a common mistake. He assumed that a company which takes steps to project a specific image, hires professionals to create such an image and spends money on promoting such an image, must necessarily be successful in what it is trying to do.

But your image does not depend on what you do, or even what you are. It depends utterly and absolutely on *what the other person thinks of you*. Mrs Raphel and I both perceived our banks to be unfriendly. The banks perceived themselves differently. But self-perception does not count: it is the other person's perception which determines your image.

Simple though it sounds, this is the central secret of all successful image-building activities. And since all this is leading on to how you should develop your personal image with a view to growing rich, let me spell it out just one more time in these words:

Image is in the Eye of the Beholder

Before you take any steps to build, project or change your image, imagine how it looks from the other person's viewpoint.

Imagine how it looks from the other person's viewpoint . . . that's the fundamental secret. And when you start to think about the fundamental secret, you're very quickly led to another secret, even more important. I call it the Chameleon Secret and what it comes down to is this:

No one image is right for everything.

Let's get right down to practicalities here. In the last chapter I told you that your first step on the road to riches was to get yourself a job. Let's assume you've taken my advice and have been scouring the Situations Vacant columns for something suitable. Let's further assume you've found something that interests you: a post with Rank Xerox selling copiers. The ad asks you to write supplying details of your previous experience.

You will recall that in the last chapter I also gave you an example of a letter virtually guaranteed to get you as far as an interview. Maybe you sent that letter, or maybe you showed a little initiative and wrote one of your own. Either way, the assumption is that the Rank Xerox Recruitment Officer (whose signature you can't decipher) has asked you to come in for an interview. You are now deciding what sort of image you should project when you get there.

What's it going to be? Friendly? Efficient? Businesslike? Formal? Tough? Conservative? Or what? The thing to do is sit down and think carefully about which one suits you best—right?

Wrong! The thing to do is find out which one suits *Rank*

Xerox best. Or, more accurately, which one suits that mysterious Recruitment Officer best. *Image is in the Eye of the Beholder*. It's how he sees you that counts, not how you see yourself or even how you *want* to see yourself.

From this it follows that successfully projecting a personal image is actually:

The art of manipulating others to see what you want them to see. So how do you go about manipulating the Recruitment Officer?

The first thing you do is find out his name. Nobody earns Brownie Points for an interview which starts out 'Well, Mr Um-um . . .' If you can't read his writing, lift the phone before you're called for interview and *find out*. And since you've paid for the call, maximize the return on your investment by finding out as much as possible about him. How old is he (roughly)? What level of management does he represent? Is he solely a Recruitment Officer or does he dovetail these responsibilities with others? Will he make the employment decision or simply recommend to someone else?

Questions like these look heavy when written down, but a friendly chat with a receptionist will normally elicit the information you need without too much difficulty. It is information you will soon put to good use.

Remember you are trying to manipulate the Recruitment Officer to see what you want him to see. To do this, you must imagine yourself in his place. Ask yourself if you were this Recruitment Officer, what sort of candidate would impress you?

Here you need to use a good deal of common sense. There are no set answers to this sort of question. You need to use the information you have and analyze the situation carefully. Bear in mind that however much you manage to find out in advance, you may still wish to modify your approach when you meet the man face to face.

Let's look at some (but by no means all) of the areas you might like to consider.

First, in my chauvinist way, I have used the male pronoun throughout my examples, but there is a solid chance that the Recruitment Officer will be female. If you, dear reader, are female too, you will have no problems with this situation. But if you are male you may have some difficulty putting yourself in the Recruitment Officer's place. Try to remember that even now women in business have a harder time than men. Despite the liberation and the legislation, prejudice is rife and much of it is all the worse because it is unconscious. The average woman in business has to be a whole lot brighter, work a whole lot harder just to be accorded the same level of opportunity as her male counterparts. Despite the myths, women in management did not get where they are by sleeping with the boss. They made it on ability and talent. Remember this if your interviewer is female. She will not take kindly to being patronized, or charmed, or shown your hairy chest in some lunatic attempt to stimulate her hormones. Leave the macho act at the door and manipulate her by being *businesslike*. It should prove so refreshingly unusual that she may well offer you the job on the spot.

Sex aside, you should always remember that your interviewer is a person with personal concerns. An older executive, nearing retirement, may welcome a whiz kid into the firm. A younger man, if he is insecure, may worry that someone as energetic as you could end up with his job. You need to read the man or the woman, and pitch your image accordingly.

You can see now why I call this the Chameleon Secret. The little lizard changes colour in relation to its background. To become successful, you need to change your image in relation to your situation, your specific goals and the individuals involved.

But while all this is very well in theory, how do you project an image *in practice*? Let's have a look at the more important components of the art.

Projecting an Image

First, clothes.

A highly conservative colleague of mine, Joint Managing Director of a large, successful company, once told me about a young American woman who applied to him for a job. She arrived for the interview dressed in the most outrageous clothing he had ever seen: casual, colourful, sloppy, bizarre.

While he was still reeling from the initial impression, she compounded the sin by rolling herself a cigarette and striking a match on the seat of her jeans!

Did she get the job? Indeed she did. The company involved was an advertising agency, the job was in the creative department. In the advertising industry, creative people are *expected* to dress outlandishly and behave peculiarly. (Indeed, such characteristics are often mistaken for talent.) Thus the applicant had applied the Chameleon Secret and projected the appropriate image.

The rule of dress is simple: *Dress appropriately and as well as you can afford*.

The latter part of that rule is interesting. Books really are judged by their covers and people all too often by the way they dress. The appropriateness of your attire is directly related to the Chameleon Secret, but the *quality* of your attire is related to nothing other than itself. It should, quite simply, be the best you can manage: a habit which will stand you in excellent stead on your road to riches.

And when you consider what constitutes the best you can manage, remember that image is *perception*, not actuality. A friend of my wife managed for years to project a quality image by rummaging through the clothing stalls at jumble sales for anything (however tatty) with a designer label. She would then carefully unpick the *labels* and sew then onto her own clothes.

But as that last little anecdote might suggest, clothes can only take you part of the way. Despite her labels, Flora (my wife's friend) could not have projected her image so successfully without the correct *attitude*.

Here again, we are deeply embedded in the Chameleon Secret, for the correct attitude is always relative to the circumstances. To judge attitude, put yourself in the other person's place and imagine what attitude would sit best from that viewpoint . . . then put yourself back in your own place and adopt it!

There are, however, certain characteristics which are almost universally useful to project in image terms. One is relaxation. Another is enthusiasm. And another is interest—specifically, interest in the other person.

Since we are, at this stage at least, speaking of image primarily in terms of netting yourself a job, it is as well to know that the executive who interviews you is often as nervous as you are. (The decision he makes will, after all, cost his company many thousands of pounds over the years.) Nervousness is communicative. If two people are exhibiting nervous signs, a sort of negative oscillation begins which swiftly makes both extremely uncomfortable with one another. Even where only one party shows nervousness, it calls up a negative response in the other.

But what you *feel* need not necessarily be what you *project*. Hide your nervousness and project relaxation.

Enthusiasm works in the opposite direction to nervousness in that it calls up a very positive response in most people. The trick is well known to salespeople who work very hard to become enthusiastic about their product. Projected enthusiasm about the job you are seeking will always predispose an interviewer to think well of you. Even generalized enthusiasm will often do the trick, on the premise that someone enthusiastic about life will tend to be equally enthusiastic about his work.

Interest is a little more tricky to project. In an interview situation, you are aiming, among other things, for memorability. To achieve it, you need to remember that your interviewer is neither a god nor a Martian, but a human being like yourself. And as a human being, the one thing that interests him most is . . . himself. And by taking an interest in the one thing that interests him most, you capture his attention.

This is an approach which needs a light touch, however. Any hint of prying or pushing your interest too far will meet with immediate rejection. You can achieve the necessary balance by allowing the other person to make the running.

The Seven Sure-Fire Steps to Getting a Job

Let's list what we've learned for easy reference. You'll find it adds up to seven sure-fire steps to netting a job.

1. Remember that image is in the eye of the beholder.
2. Decide the overall style of image most suited to the given situation.
3. Find out all you can about the executive who will interview you.
4. Use the Chameleon Secret: tailor your image to the situation you confront and the person you wish to influence.
5. Project relaxation.
6. Project enthusiasm.
7. Project interest.

For someone who clearly advocates that you should work for yourself, I've now spent an inordinate amount of space on telling you how to get yourself a job. But there is method in the madness, for employment should never be considered an end in itself, but rather as an asset to be exploited.

This is an interesting point and one that bears some thought. Few workers ever consider their employment as an asset; and consequently few workers ever attempt to capitalize upon it. Yet experience quickly indicates the asset value of employment. Try raising a mortgage if you are unemployed. Or raising a loan. Or even negotiating a smallish overdraft.

These observations are by no means academic. When you begin to work for yourself, you are going to need *capital*. And unless you have a rich uncle in precarious health, the chances are that the capital can only come from one of two sources: savings or borrowings.

Both are a lot easier if you have a job.

8
HOW TO BEAT THE BANK

Since the varieties of human nature are infinite, there must, I suppose, be millionaires somewhere who keep their money in a sock. But not, I suspect, many. Wealth and banking go together, so that if you are stepping on the road to riches, it is certainly useful to know something about the banking system . . . specifically, how to beat it.

Banks, as we have already remarked, are prone to lend you money only when you do not need it. With equal frequency they time their best offer on deposit interest rates to coincide with those periods when you have nothing to invest. They project an image of security while operating on perilously shaky foundations. They open, by and large, at highly inconvenient hours.

Few other industries could get away with this sort of nonsense. But then few other industries strike terror into the hearts of their customers. This is achieved through the exploitation of the banking industry's greatest asset: a centuries old mystique seldom questioned by the person in the street. But if you are to use the banking system effectively— that is, to your personal advantage—it is not only vital that you *do* question that mystique, but also that you abolish it from your own thinking completely.

The History of Banking

Banking is a profession as old as prostitution, with which it shares certain characteristics. Little is known in detail of the industry prior to the thirteenthth century but it is possible to divide the earliest 'bankers' into two main groups.

One group was the coin and bullion merchants. In an age when communications were poor and travel difficult, those who required foreign exchange had problems. The bullion merchants went into business to solve these problems. They operated as money changers and supplied foreign (and domestic) coin of a guaranteed weight and quality.

The second group—forerunner of our present system—was the merchant bankers, a breed who are with us still. In the early days, the emphasis was on *merchant*, for banking was actually only a small aspect of their business.

Such merchants traded internationally and often maintained assets at different points along the established trading routes. If you or I needed to pay out money to someone in, say, Jamaica, we could save ourselves the trouble and expense of sailing there by paying the money to an international merchant, who would then instruct his agent in Jamaica to pay your creditor out of local funds. Since the merchant who carried out this service was not a charitable institution, he expected a little something for his trouble. Initially, the little something would derive from currency exchange. The merchant would accept your payment in honest English sovereigns and, if the situation permitted, pay your creditor in cowrie shells. But bankers were as greedy then as they are now and the profits which accrued on foreign exchange soon proved insufficient to satisfy them. They cast about for ways of charging you interest.

Interest charges, in mediaeval times, were known by the biblical name of *usury* and were universally held to be both sinful and illegal. (Today, of course, they are a way of life.) The early bankers introduced a system of deferred payment which cunningly disguised the fact of interest charges and, one assumes, sorted out the sinful aspect at Confession.

That other fundamental aspect of modern banking, the

taking of deposits, was largely developed in England in the seventeenth century. At that time there existed a class of people known as *money scriveners*, notaries who had come to specialize in bringing together people who might usefully do business with one another, including potential borrowers and lenders. Since not all business deals were noted for an abundance of trust, the scrivener would often accept deposits of money as part of his service.

Experience soon showed something rather odd about these deposits. Once a number of people made them, a fund was created which had a mysterious tendency towards stability: withdrawals were generally balanced by deposits, generating a pool of idle cash. Although this cash was not, of course, theirs, the scriveners were quick to see its profit potential and began to lend it out at interest (usury by then having become far more socially acceptable).

The scriveners began to do so well from this enterprise that they attracted the attention of the London goldsmiths. Goldsmiths require secure vaults for their raw material and as a sideline had long hired out space in their vaults to customers for the safekeeping of money and valuables. Now the scriveners had shown this money on deposit could be turned into a valuable asset, the goldsmiths did a very clever thing: they ceased to charge for the safekeeping of cash and actually offered to pay interest on any left with them. Naturally the interest they paid out was far below the interest the money would earn for them, but the scriveners never really figured out what was happening. As a result, more and more money accrued to the goldsmiths (who evolved eventually into modern bankers), while the scriveners went the way of the dodo.

At about the same time as embryonic banks were discovering that you did not need to own money to make money, customers were discovering that you could transfer part of a credit balance to a third party by writing an instruction to your goldsmith/bank. Such written instructions were not yet called cheques, but cheques they were none the less.

Once cheques started to fly around, of course, it took the goldsmiths only an eyeblink to figure that customers might enjoy *borrowing* by cheque as well: a loan account might be debited with an amount borrowed which was then deposited into a current account on which customers could draw by cheque. Alternatively, a customer might be permitted to *overdraw* his account (using the newfangled cheques) to an agreed amount. Either way, interest could be charged to the customer. Before you could say *usury*, every goldsmith in London was at the practice. And like bubonic plague, it spread.

In 1661, the Bank of Stockholm discovered a new way of defrauding its customers for profit. It issued Europe's first banknote. (Europe's, but not the world's: that doubtful distinction, like so many others, goes to China.)

These banknotes were certificates of claim against the bank itself, documents which promised faithfully to pay the bearer a certain sum of gold or silver. Since even then banks were determined to start out as they meant to go on, these notes were issued on two criteria only: how much money the public was likely to want at a given time; and how confident the public was in the bank's ability to meet its commitments. Notable for its absence was what the average person might consider a third and in every way most important criterion: the *actual* ability of the bank to meet its pledges.

In fact, virtually from the first banknote issue, no bank was actually in a position to meet the totality of its pledges. Banknotes were a lie . . . but a lie that would never be found out unless everybody decided to cash in their chips at once—an occurrence deemed (rightly) to be unlikely.

When the banknote experiment proved such a resounding success, banks went into the creation of money in an even bigger way by permitting customers overdraft facilities which not only exceeded what funds were available to the customer, but also what funds were available to the bank itself. In other words, the totality of loans issued (which reached out into the world of trade and commerce in the form of cheques) exceeded the bank's ability to pay at any given time. Nobody worried, least of all the banks. The Banknote Syndrome had taught bankers they were unlikely to be caught out. Besides, with more money in circulation in whatever form, everybody was a little richer, a little happier. An early ancestor of Harold Macmillan might reasonably have told the population they had never had it so good.

The Banking System Today

A study of the history of banking presents a salutory lesson in deception, ingenuity, ruthlessness and greed; and by so doing performs the useful service of stripping away the myth of respectability which surrounds the banking industry today.

And myth it is, for the situation has changed little in its fundamentals since the days we have been discussing . . . and what changes there are have generally been for the worse.

Take a moment now to *read* a £5 note. When you decipher the ornate and impressive writing, you will find the words, 'I promise to pay the bearer on demand the sum of five pounds.' You will also find the signature of the Chief Cashier of the Bank of England. In other words, what you hold in your hand is still a promissory note, just like those issued by the Bank of Stockholm. The difference is that in the early days the promise meant something (however little, however insecure). Today it means nothing at all so far as I can ascertain in discussions with a variety of bankers. The *pound* referred to in the early notes was a pound weight of precious metal, e.g. gold. Later, it became a 'pound's worth' of the same metal—whatever a 'pound's worth' meant. Since the Gold Standard was abandoned, even this gossamer tie-line to reality was broken. Present your £5 note to a bank today and demand the promise be honoured and the chances are high that a call will be put through for a squad of burly men in white coats. *Nobody* pays any attention to the promise on the banknotes any more: we are collectively involved in a conspiracy of belief so fundamental and so widespread that the economic base of our entire civilization would collapse if we abandoned it.

If banknotes are essentially meaningless, it is as well to point out that the situation with regard to deposits has not changed much either: the day when all depositors want their money back at once is the day the bank goes down the tubes.

It is enlightening to read the definitive definition of a commercial banker (as given in the *Encyclopaedia Britannica*):

'A commercial banker is a dealer in money and substitutes for money, such as cheques or bills of exchange. He also provides a variety of financial services.

'The basis of his business is borrowing from individuals, firms and occasionally government—i.e., receiving "deposits" from them. With these resources and also with his own capital, the banker makes loans or extends credit and also invests in securities . . .'

The importance of all this is its value as an attitudinal corrective. Almost all of us are nervous of banks, which appear to be institutions of overwhelming power and propriety. And since nervousness is definitely counterproductive in beating the bank, it is important to understand that, contrary to their public image, banks are businesses with a buccaneering tradition, a shady past and a distinctly questionable present. Anyone who learns that and stays nervous needs his head examined.

How to Make the Banking System Work for You

It was a banker who introduced me to the art of *kiting*.

The principles of kiting are relatively simple and since they have now been made virtually obsolete by computerization, I have little hesitation in spelling them out here.

Kiting worked at a time when inter-bank communication was slow and a cheque took three days minimum to clear. To fly a kite, what you did was this.

Starting on Monday morning at 10 a.m., you presented yourself at Goldsmith's Bank in Main Street and opened a current (cheque book) account with £100 cash. (The actual sum is relatively unimportant, but £100 makes calculations easier.) This done, you walked round to Scrivener's Bank in High Street and open a second current account *using a cheque for £100 drawn on Goldsmith's*.

If we pause for a moment here, you will see you have done nothing illegal. Your account with Goldsmith's is genuine and you have sufficient funds to meet the £100 cheque you just issued. If there is a query, Scrivener's can ring Goldsmith's and quickly confirm everything is in order.

So now you have a current account at Scrivener's with £100 in credit and a current account at Goldsmiths's with a credit balance of zero. Or have you? Since we are discussing a time when cheques took three days to clear, it will be Wednesday at the very earliest before the cheque you drew on Goldsmith's is actually presented. Thus, on paper, at 10.30 a.m. on Monday, you have not one but *two* current accounts, each in credit to the tune of £100.

Now you take your new Scrivener cheque book and make your way back to Goldsmith's. Write a cheque for £100 on your Scrivener account and deposit it into your Goldsmith account. This leaves you with £200 in your Goldsmith account, but since, as we have already remarked, the cheque you issued will take three working days to clear, you still have—at least on paper—£100 in Scriveners. It is still not 11 o'clock on Monday morning and already you have kited your original £100 into £300 so far as bank records are concerned. But as we have already seen, bank records have long since taken the place of reality where money is concerned, so for the time being you are perfectly entitled to regard yourself as £200 better off.

This is, however, only a very small start. You have become, temporarily at least, a professional cheque-casher. Each time you visit one bank from now on, you will deposit a cheque for the full amount shown on paper to be credited to your other account. Assume that by close of business on Monday, you have managed to visit one of the two banks and carry out this transaction every half an hour. By 3 p.m. your total worth between the two bank accounts is a staggering £8,900.

Most people find it hard to believe you could ever have converted £100 into close on £9,000 in a single day, whatever system you were using. But if you care to work it through on the basis of transactions at 10 a.m., 10.30 a.m., 11 a.m., 11.30 a.m., 12 noon, 12.30 p.m., 1.30 p.m., 2 p.m., 2.30 p.m., and 3 p.m., you will find the figure accurate enough—and nothing like as impressive as the figures you are about to generate on the following day's work.

Since none of your cheques is due to clear before Wednesday, you can start the whole thing up again on Tuesday morning at Goldsmith's by writing a £5,500 cheque on Scrivener's.

Assuming once again that you manage a transaction every half an hour through the banking day, you will, (believe it or not) end the day with £418,100 in your account at Goldsmith's and an even more satisfying £676,500 stashed away at Scriveners . . . over £1,000,000 to your credit for only two day's work.

Of course when Wednesday dawns, the cheques you wrote on Monday will start to clear. But since the *total* cheques you wrote on Monday amount to less than £9,000, they will make a very small dent in your overall total. And if you continue to transact as before on Wednesday, you have nothing to worry about when Tuesday's cheques are presented either. In fact so long as you keep your kite flying, your worth, so far as these two banks are concerned, will continue to grow.

But what happens if you stop? What happens if you simply cease to deposit cheques from one account to the other?

What happens is that over a period of days, your paper millions will dwindle down to your original £100 float, less various bank charges.

Before quitting your career as a professional cheque-casher, you might, however, liquidate the twin accounts and head for Bermuda (or, more realistically, some warm South American country lacking extradition treaties with the remainder of the world). This sort of action would be totally illegal, of course, but raising credit with a third bank—or with a Rolls Royce salesman—might not be. Most credit checks are carried out on your bank account and you would have two in a very healthy state indeed.

Kiting, alas, is not what it used to be. Indeed, most bankers assure me that the simple scheme I have just outlined would never have worked since it is far too open and a banker would have to be deaf, dumb and blind not to realize what was going on. Genuine kiting (which follows the same essential principles) did go on, however, especially in situations where it could be disguised within heavy genuine cash flows. Thus it was a business game, not something carried out by the little old lady around the corner.

Today the improvement in inter-bank communications has made kiting virtually impossible, but it has not changed one of the most important principles of beating the bank—the importance of maintaining two or more accounts in different banks.

The reason for this is associated with banking's most carefully guarded secret.

Banking's Most Carefully Guarded Secret

Years ago I was as much in awe of bankers as anyone. Then one sunny Thursday afternoon I walked unexpectedly (and unannounced) into the home of my next door neighbour and found her making love to my bank manager on the kitchen floor.

The trauma was sufficient to change my image of bankers forever. (And somewhat change my image of my next door neighbour). Fate had delivered me the most carefully guarded of all banking secrets, a secret so vital, so fundamental to success that you might care to engrave it in granite. It is a secret which can be expressed in just three words:

Bankers are human.

A great many benefits flow directly from this realization. Perhaps the most important is the recognition that the way banking is carried on does not depend on obscure and difficult financial calculations, but rather on human nature. And human nature is always open to manipulation.

How to Approach a Banker

Bankers are generally approached with deference, nervousness, timidity or aggression—at least when one seeks a loan. None of these approaches is ideal in any circumstances and may, in many circumstances, actually prove counterproductive.

When you start on the premise that your banker is human, however, it permits the creation of a totally different environment. Earlier we discussed image and how the projection of a successful image depended absolutely on your ability to put yourself in the other person's place. Essentially the same thing applies to a successful visit to your bank manager. Take the trouble to put yourself in his place.

Once you do this, even a loan application falls into its proper perspective. The £3,000 you plan to ask for (not to mention the £5,000 you actually need) may mean financial life and death to you. To your banker, whose total professional responsibilities run to millions, it is a flea-bite.

In a later chapter we will go into much more detail on the art of raising bankloans. What we are studying here is the more generalized manipulation of your bankers, the sort of approach that makes them like you, appreciate you, think kindly of you and consequently treat you well.

This approach is based totally and absolutely on the continuing conscious realization that you are dealing with a human being who eats, sleeps and excretes exactly as you do, who worries about decreasing opportunity and increasing waistline, whose childen are a drain on resources, emotional and financial, whose spouse may be unfaithful . . . and who may actually be in love with your next door neighbour.

Treat this person as a fellow human being and doors will open to you. I will not pretend you will automatically get everything you could possibly wish for, but I will positively guarantee you will be treated better by your bankers than the average customer is.

Beyond this generalized good treatment—and the un-doubted pleasure of cementing another human relationship which may well prove of benefit to you in the years ahead—you can used your new-found realization of the banker's humanity to apply subtle pressures.

One of these pressures is to make certain you have more than one account, each in competitive banks. Bankers hate this—I have met several who tried to leave me with the impression it was actually *illegal*—but it stops them taking you for granted. Competitive situations usually work in favour of the consumer, which in this instance is you.

I have noticed that when you seek to open an account, you are invariably asked if you have an account elsewhere. This is a fortunate habit, since it not only saves you the trouble of raising the matter, but permits you a little one-upmanship as well. The only realistic answer to whether you have an account elsewhere is Yes, whether this happens to be true or not. And when you are asked where, answer 'Zurich'. Swiss banking being what it is, your claim is uncheckable. The reputation of Swiss banking being what it is, your claim is also very impressive indeed. This evocation of the Gnomes of Zurich might even, if skilfully done, earn you an overdraft.

The Importance of Banking

The importance of banking to you on your road to riches is not so much that it will provide you with a safe haven for your millions when you make them, but rather that it will aid you in the money-making process.

Banks, as we have seen, exist to speculate with your money when you have it and loan you money at exorbitant rates of interest when you do not. You will eventually need to borrow money in order to fund your get-rich schemes and banks are an excellent source.

Before you reach that stage, however, it may be as well to discover what sort of get-rich schemes are most suited to your particular talents. In my next chapter, I am going to make the assumption that you are in employment, comfortably off but not necessarily solvent and determined to grab yourself a much larger slice of the financial cake than you are eating now.

And on those assumptions, I plan to show you how to do just that.

9
MANUFACTURING YOUR MONEY MACHINE

Everything you've read up to now has been important . . . but preliminary. But this is the moment you've been waiting for: the moment when you set about building your personal *money machine*, the business that is going to carry you (hopefully, at speed) from your present state of penury to wealth, comfort and success.

You will not, of course, be the first to create such a machine. Many others have trod the Royal Road to El Dorado. But if you pause to examine their progress, you will find they frequently took different *routes*.

J. Paul Getty made his money in the oil business. Howard Hughes accumulated wealth in the aeroplane industry. Henry Ford got rich manufacturing motor cars. Tony O'Reilly is a baked bean baron. Some members of the Vanderbilt dynasty made it big in banking. Gloria Vanderbilt, however, earns a crust by marketing designer jeans. Aristotle Onassis was a shipping magnate. And so on in an almost bewildering diversity.

The question is, which route should you take?

Avoiding the Most Commonplace Mistake

A lot of would-be millionaires fail for a reason you might find it hard to believe: they go into business without *thinking*, without ever stopping to consider if the line of business contemplated is actually right for them. It happens like this.

They leave school or college and find a job that happens to be available, or well paid, or convenient. After a few years they decide to branch out on their own. They're determined to make a lot of money, so they read up on successful people, maybe talk to a few personally. They try to find the magic formulae for success and very quickly they discover most successful people attribute their wealth to two major factors.

The first is hard work and long hours. The second is business and market experience.

Everyone with a genuine interest in making money is prepared to work for long hours. But it is that second factor which sinks the ship. It sounds reasonable that you are going to succeed best in an area of which you have experience, so nine budding entrepreneurs out of ten *try to set up in the same line of business they have worked in as an employee* . This *can* be okay. But it can also be the biggest mistake you'll ever make. Remember you took up a particular type of employment for reasons which have nothing whatever to do with its potential as a business.

This is such an important point, I want to take just a little space to enlarge on it. A good business looks very different from employer and employee viewpoints. From the employee viewpoint, a business is good if it pays high salaries or wages, demands little in the way of effort, offers prospect of upward mobility, provides security and a clean, safe, pleasant place to work.

From the employer viewpoint, a good business is one that makes the maximum amount of money.

When you stop to think about it, almost all the things that are important to an employee—high wages, pleasant conditions, small demands, pension schemes—detract from the bottom line return of the employer.

So chances are that the sort of business that attracted you as an employee will NOT be the sort of business which would make most money for you if you were running it for yourself.

Where does that leave the question of experience? Let me say up front that gaining experience *is* important. But the emphasis is firmly on that word *gaining*. Experience is something you gain in the marketplace. And the market experience gained by the boss is frequently something very different from the market experience gained by the employee—even in the same business.

What I am saying here is very simple: don't be afraid of lack of experience. Accept that you will make mistakes. But accept too that you must *learn* by your mistakes. The most valuable of all experience is learning by your mistakes. If you do this, persevere and refuse to be beaten, you will succeed in the long run. And that's guaranteed!

Selecting Your Best Business Bet

So if experience is no longer the definitive criterion, how should you go about selecting the business that will turn on your money machine? Let's examine the six golden rules for selecting the style of business that will have every chance of working well for you.

1. The Golden Rule of Excitement
Select a business that excites you. Millions have been made in the oil business, but if the oil business bores you, don't touch it with a barge-pole. Nobody ever yawned their way to wealth. A vital ingredient in the formula for success (some would say *the* vital ingredient) is enthusiasm. If you don't have it, you won't make it. Furthermore, enthusiasm is something you will certainly need to carry you over the early setbacks. Because there *will* be setbacks and your overall strategy must take note of them.

2. The Golden Rule of Timing
One of the most harrowing cautionary tales you will ever hear in business concerns the man who invested heavily in a company making buggy whips . . . the same day the first

model T Ford rolled off the production line. It's a very old story, but the moral is as relevant as ever. Make sure the business you go into stands a real chance of success right here, right now.

Right here means the country or district where you plan to set up your business. Fur-lined jackets may be a hot seller in downtown New York in winter, but you won't move many to a Bedouin in the middle of the desert.

Right now means the present day and age, realistically viewed. Maybe you're thinking of exporting a new, improved set of coveralls designed for production line workers in the Japanese car industry. Sounds great—and at one time it would have *been* great. Right now, however, there are fewer and fewer production line workers in the Japanese car industry: the work is mainly done by robots. Your idea is targetted into a rapidly shrinking market.

3. The Golden Rule of Relevance

I know a great many people very anxious to make a killing in business. Most of them look for what they call *creative* ways of doing it. They search the world for novel products—microchip-based toasters that play you a different tune each morning for three months, a combined knife/fork/spoon guaranteed to halve the washing-up in an average household—and in just about every case they fail miserably to make much money.

The reason, quite simply, is that their products are not *relevant* to the basic needs of the market at which they are aimed. (The knife/fork/spoon set might be relevant to campers, but not to a domestic family market.)

Let me tell you a true story. Judy Challen is an elderly Australian lady who loved everything about her husband except one thing: he snored. Since this kept her awake night after night, she passed the time by watching him sleep. And in doing so, she noticed something interesting: he only snored when his head lay in certain positions.

So Judy experimented with a pillow specially shaped so that it kept his head out of the positions which made him snore. She persuaded her husband to try it and his snoring stopped! Naturally she told the story of her achievement to neighbours and before long the inevitable happened: a sleepy friend asked Judy to make up a second special pillow to shut up *her* snoring husband. Judy did and the pillow worked again. Silent Knight pillows, the trade name adopted by the company which markets Judy's marvellous invention, now sell by the thousands in Australia and are, at the time of writing, moving with every indication of even greater success into the international market-place.

The point about this story is that Judy invented a much *needed* product. Vast numbers of people snore and vast numbers of their spouses lie awake at night gnashing their teeth and listening. This situation creates a *need* and a *market*. There is little *need* for a singing toaster, so its *market* is confined to novelty sales. *If you offer a needed product or service at a fair price to a wide market, you will do well*.

Like every rule, there are exceptions. The very rich comprise a target market in themselves and may certainly be sold non-essential vulgarities like solid gold bath taps. But the competition for their attention is fierce and it is worth remembering that most rich people got that way by being careful with money, not by spending it foolishly!

4. *The Golden Rule of Knowledge*

Avoid starting up a business you know nothing about. We're not talking *experience* here—I've already had my say on that topic—we're talking knowledge.

A good friend of mine once decided he would start up a weekly newspaper. He had no experience of the field, which was okay because expertise can always be bought, but he had no real *knowledge* of it either.

As a businessman, however, he could not see how it would fail. He had selected a prosperous, heavily-populated and fast-growing business town which did not yet have a weekly newspaper of its own, and carried out market research which indicated a newspaper would be welcomed by readers and was badly needed as an advertising vehicle for local businesses. The indications could not have been more positive. He set up an office, negotiated a deal with a printer, created a format, collected material for his first issue and announced its imminent publication in a fanfare of local publicity.

Two weeks before the launch date he called me in for last minute advice and I warned him his entire venture was set for disaster. I was no better businessman than he was—and indeed agreed with his business assessment of the prospects—but I had considerable knowledge of local newspapers, having worked in the field for many years. To save capital and running costs, my friend had not hired any editorial staff: he proposed to put the publication together himself with the help of freelances. This sounded reasonable enough since he had previous experience of monthly magazines and was a skilled editor. But he also proposed to sell advertising for the newspaper himself, on the pattern of old-time local newspaper editor/proprietors in the United States.

It was in this area I foresaw the problems. Editing a monthly magazine is a leisurely process compared to editing a weekly paper. (I know: I've done both.) Once you start a weekly paper, you start a tight deadline merry-go-round that simply never stops. There is scarcely time to get the editorial content together, let alone sell advertising on the side.

But what about the old-timers in America? I agreed that there had been many instances in which one man put together a weekly paper and sold advertising too. But this pattern almost always emerged in an *established* paper where the systems were virtually self-sustaining. To try to double up in a launch situation was a different thing entirely.

My friend listened politely enough, but he was too deeply committed to change his plans. He launched on deadline and closed down three months later.

Knowledge of the venture you are entering is more precious than diamonds. Far too many entrepreneurs are attracted to the glamour of a specific business, or, like my friend to its money-making potential. In such circumstances, it is all too easy to forget to check the nuts and bolts of the venture. If you don't know the business yourself, find somebody who does and spend time learning—*before* you commit yourself.

5. *The Golden Rule of Going It Alone*
This is the rule with the most exceptions. By Going It Alone, I mean setting up your own business as opposed to buying a franchise and in this whole area it is difficult to generalize. However . . . there are very real benefits to a good franchise deal. You start out with a proven product. You learn the systems that worked well elsewhere. You save money on originating decor, print material and so on. In many instances you benefit from national advertising, promotion and publicity generated and paid for by the franchise principal.

A franchise (provided it is a *known* franchise and not some fly-by-night scheme backed by Cowboy Enterprises Ltd) is almost always a more secure business proposition than going it alone. And there have been individuals who became very wealthy indeed within a franchise situation. But my experience is that these franchisee millionaires were usually in the novel position of introducing a highly successful *overseas* franchise into their own country.

My bottom line feeling is that accepting a franchise is only a step removed from the dynamics of employment. However much money you make from the deal, the company who sold you the franchise will always make more. Why work to make somebody else rich? Shoot for the moon and go it alone.

6. *The Golden Rule of Minimum Investment*
Since vast numbers of businesses go to the wall through under-capitalization, don't misread this one. We're not talking about setting up without money. Nor are we talking about

setting up without *sufficient* money. What we're talking about is wasting money on *non-essentials*. If you invest only in what is essential and ignore the frills, you will have followed the Golden Rule of Minimum Investment to the letter.

Before we leave this one, let's try to define *frills*.

The first place to look to keep your expenses down is staff. For every service business and quite a few manufacturing and marketing businesses as well, the wage bill represents by far the largest single capital outlay. Ask yourself if you really need all those people, starting with the secretary that every business person (particularly business*man*) 'has to have'. If you learn to type and can answer your own phone, you will not only save money in the vital early days, but you will also keep a closer check on what is happening in your business.

Some companies—in the Public Relations industry, for example—require strong image projection by their very nature. But unless you have decided to go into this style of business, the chances are you can survive on second-hand office furniture without wall-to-wall carpeting.

Once you go into business, of course, you become the (legitimate) target of many other businesses. Salespeople will try to persuade you that survival is impossible without a photocopier, a postage meter, a computerized telephone exchange, an electric pencil sharpener and the contract services of a solicitor and accountant. For most new businesses in their early days, none of this is true. Make your minimum possible investment in the frills and save your capital for the things that are *really* important . . . like keeping your business afloat over the bad times.

The Ethical Set-up

Since I'm assuming you have taken my advice and are starting out from a base of employment, there is another factor which you are going to have to take into consideration: whether to begin your new business venture on a full-time or a part-time basis. Both have their own dynamics, but the latter has an ethical aspect as well.

If you decide to start your new business on a part-time basis, you create for yourself an automatic temptation: the temptation to work on *your* business in your *employer's* time. I am no arbiter of your ethics, but I can tell you that, ethics apart, this is a mug's game.

Setting up a business, full-or part-time, requires your undivided attention—something difficult to give if you are looking over your shoulder wondering whether your employer will discover what you are doing.

If, as I have assumed, you are in employment when you decide to launch your new business, you have two viable choices. The first is to set your plans, leave your employment and start up. The other is to launch your new business as a weekend or night-time venture.

Which of these routes you select is up to you. Both have benefits. The first permits a clean break and a total commitment. The second allows you to spread your risk, refresh your capital and proceed at a more leisurely pace to build up your wealth. Either way, the choice is yours and there is no right or wrong approach.

Getting Rich Quick

An advertising agency in the country where I live coined a slogan for a building society client seeking new investors. The slogan was: GET RICH SLOWLY.

The advice is good for entrepreneurs as well. Even the best ideas, harnessed to the best structures, seldom generate immediate wealth. In business as in the entertainment industry, 'overnight success' usually arises after fifteen or twenty years hard work. In all the various psychological formulae for success, the most frequently forgotten element is *patience*.

However sensible this may sound, it is a good bet that even

someone as sensible as you might be tempted towards a get rich quick approach, usually at the behest of companies which promise instant wealth if you are prepared to sell their products ... the catch being that before you *sell* their products, you first have to *buy* them, usually in considerable quantities.

It is only fair to say that some companies (perhaps even many companies) who actively search out agents as part of their marketing strategies are perfectly legitimate. Nobody would question the bona fides of Tupperware or Avon Cosmetics, for example. But if you move beyond such well-known names, you move into the sort of territory where they wrote 'Here be Dragons' on the old maps.

The dragons you need to watch out for are the companies which promise huge returns on items you manufacture using the materials, kits and so on that they supply. (A more recent version of the same approach promises big money from envelope stuffing.) There is usually a strong suggestion, if not an outright promises, that the company concerned will *buy from you* everything you produce. The way the ads are worded, it sounds as if you can't lose.

I dare say there are genuine operators in this sort of area, but there are also outfits whose sole purpose in life is to make money from suckers. You purchase the raw materials, make up the particular product, then find, when you go to sell it to the company that it is 'not quite up to standard'. And however hard you try, it never will be quite up to standard since the company has no interest whatsoever in buying from you, only in selling you more raw materials.

I have no wish to make you paranoid: going into business on your own will create enough problems for you without that. But I do want to tell you that if you see a set-up-in-business offer that looks too good to be true, that's probably exactly what it is. Before you get involved in anything of this nature—manufacturing from supplied kits, direct sales, party sales or the like—*check it out*. And when you have checked it out, check it out again. Remember, it's not just your money they could be stealing, but your future, because the more time you waste on a shaky proposition, the less you will have to spend on setting up your own soundly based business.

Mail Order Millions

Of all the get-rich-quick schemes you are likely to hear about, the most fascinating is likely to be mail order selling. And while self-start ads which promise you mail order millions are likely to be no more than hooks for the latest con, I have to confess it is entirely possible to make good money from direct mail. Furthermore, I know of no business which is more exciting, more outright *fun*. And you can often set up in mail order for far less capital than any comparable business.

But it's tricky and if you are going that route, you will benefit greatly from a little practical advice—which is what you will find in the next chapter.

10
THE MAIL ORDER
MINEFIELD

A few years ago, I wrote a mailing which *oversubscribed* a major sporting organization by just short of £3 million. Last year some material I wrote to promote a seminar pulled an all-time record audience and won gold as the best business-to-business mailing in Europe. Earlier this year, I learned with some satisfaction that my work had attracted two US Echo Awards in competition with some 14,000 entries worldwide.

From this, you might imagine I know a little about mail order. In fact, I know only one thing of importance: it never pays to get cocky. Despite the resounding successes mentioned above and, I am happy to report, a good many more which generated very satisfactory sales, I have also managed to set some interesting records in a different direction.

Earlier this year, I oversaw a mailing which went out to 24,000 people and produced five replies. Two years ago, material I wrote to promote another seminar caused attendance to plummet by almost 50 per cent. Six months ago, I created a mailing for a software house which produced *no replies whatsoever*—a result many marketeers would have argued to be statistically impossible.

Mail order is a minefield and however much experience you may have, however much creative talent you may generate or buy, there is no guarantee you will reach the far side in one piece. But it is a fascinating minefield and one which promises quite remarkable rewards if you get it right.

Mail order will, for example, permit you to set up in

business for less capital outlay than any other comparable enterprise I know. You may end up chauffeur-driven in the back seat of a Rolls but you can *start out* without an office, without staff, without transport, without, in fact, *any* of the expensive accoutrements which normally go with setting up a business.

Mail order permits you to export without agents, outlets or offices abroad. It enables you to select your target market with a precision the largest multi-national corporation must envy. Properly monitored, it is wholly cost-accountable so that you know precisely the returns you receive on every advertising pound. Your brightest ideas may be tested economically on a small scale and the results used to determine (to an accuracy of +/- 10 per cent) how much money you will make or lose on a major investment.

Perhaps best of all, if you find yourself with a success on your hands, you can usually repeat that success using the same material, the same advertising year by year, over and over to an expanding market.

But before you run into the minefield, it is important to get your head in order. And the first thing to realize is that mail order is not a business in itself: rather it is a *method* of *doing business*. This means that before you move a muscle, you need a product (or service) you can sell.

Selecting the Product

Nobody ever made money selling anvils mail order: the packaging is murder and the postage costs too high. Despite this, I have had personal experience of a depressingly long line of entrepreneurs who attempted to make money by mail with utterly unsuitable products.

In evaluating your product for mail order, you need to ask a series of simple questions.

1. *Will it travel by mail?* Anvils won't: that's painfully obvious. But glassware isn't a particularly good candidate either. Nor

are fresh foodstuffs. Nor are light but bulky items like beanbags or giant soft toys.

None of these things is *impossible* to sell mail order. Foodstuffs in the form of deep frozen steaks and smoked salmon are mailed across the United States daily. Ireland exports quite an amount of glass and crystalware by mail. Beanbags and soft toys are sometimes sold by mail in kit form. I even had a lecture class present me with a plan to sell mail order anvils! (You only mail the solicitation material: the customer is obliged to collect his anvil from a central store.)

But because a thing is possible does not mean it is easy or profitable. Shipping glass, for example, means your packaging, administration and insurance costs rocket. Deep freezing food needs special equipment—and special containers for dispatch. All these things increase your costs and push profit that much further away.

Your ideal product is light, durable, non-perishable, non-toxic and easily packed. That way, you keep your costs low and avoid dispatch problems.

2. *Is the product easily obtainable by your customers elsewhere?* If the answer is Yes, your answer should be No. If your potential customer can buy the *same* product at even a roughly comparable price in his local supermarket, that's exactly what he will do. He will do it because he can see the product, examine the product, maybe even try out the product before he buys. You *can* match these benefits by mail if you're clever, but there is one you can never match—immediacy. If he buys from the supermarket, he can own the product in the time it takes to get through the nearest checkout. You can only offer him delivery a day or two down the line. Make things easy for yourself. The rule is:

Never try to compete head on with established, easily obtainable lines. Your product must be novel, unusual, special, unique or difficult to obtain if it is to run any chance of success.

When you get really good at the game, you might include products which, if not particularly special in themselves, may be *presented* as special. But start out with a product that is genuinely *rare* for one reason or another. (Do remember, though, that rarity may be related to price or performance. There is nothing rare about an electric light bulb, but I saw one marketed successfully by mail on the premise that it lasted four times longer than those in the shops. And if your widget costs a fraction of the price asked by the local supermarket, you may still be able to mail it successfully.)

3. *How will my prospect see my product?* Human nature being what it is, this one can be a real killer. I have seen even the most experienced and hard-nosed direct marketeers break apart on it. Because the product excited *them* they assumed it must excite their target market. But the product usually excited *them* because of its profit potential, while the target market judged it by very different criteria.

Look at your product through the eyes of the target market. Is it genuine value for money? Do they really *need* it? Will it make life better, easier, more comfortable, more economical for them?

You may leap from your bed in the morning bursting with enthusiasm about your product, and that is understandable— it is the one thing which, hopefully, will pay your rent today and make you rich tomorrow. But as a customer, I do not share your interest and enthusiasm. I am likely to remain forever disinterested in your product unless you can give me a very strong reason indeed for paying attention. Even then, I will not see it as you do. If there is even the smallest chance that I will buy, it is because I might—just might—relate your product to the solution of one of my personal problems.

Evaluate your product from the customer's viewpoint. Put yourself in the consumer's place and don't delude yourself that he or she will see your product as you do.

4. *Can I get sufficient stocks of product?* This question sounds so childish that far too few marketeers ever bother to ask it . . . until it is too late. If you go into direct mail marketing you will be in

one of two situations: (a) marketing a product (or service) you generate yourself; or (b) marketing a product or service you buy from someone else. Either way the question is relevant. Native caution may prompt you to *underestimate* the amount of orders your mailing will generate. Generally, this is no bad thing, especially when you are calculating how much money you can afford to lose. But mail order *can* be magic and there is always the possibility of an exceptional response. In such circumstances, you *must* be geared to fulfil the orders generated—and fulfil them promptly.

You may have noticed mail order advertisements which require respondents to 'Allow 28 days for delivery'. Some at least of these disguise organizations which *carry no product stocks at all* but purchase to fulfil orders *as they arrive*. It is a nerve-wracking way of doing business, one which I believe to be unfair to customers and ultimately counter-productive in terms of profits. In mail order, as in most forms of marketing, success is spelled C-U-S-T-O-M-E-R S-A-T-I-S-F-A-C-T-I-O-N and I have yet to meet the customer who is delighted to wait until December for the product he paid for on 1 November.

Be prepared for success. Make sure your production can be switched quickly to meet maximum demand. Or if you are buying stocks elsewhere, make sure you can quickly fulfil a buoyant response. It is a simple enough rule, but one that can make a lot of difference to your business long-term.

5. *Can I make a profit on the deal?* If the last question hardly seemed worth asking, this one must be the all-time silly query? What sort of idiot would go into a mail order project without ensuring its profit potential?

Unfortunately, a great many mail order projects are structured for loss before they ever get off the ground, not because the people who mounted them were idiots, but because they were inexperienced. Mail order marketing is replete with *hidden* costs. Even its accounting procedures are alien to mainstream marketeers. There are many businesses which prosper on a margin of 1 or 2 per cent, but they are not mail order businesses.

No experienced mail order marketeer will even consider a product that does not permit a mark-up of 100 per cent. Most prefer 200 per cent and the really smart operators do not relax until they can achieve a 300 per cent mark-up.

If this sounds like competition for usury, I should stress that we are talking *mark-up* here and not profit. Look at your manufacturing or purchase costs. Mark them up by an *absolute minimum* of 100 per cent and ask yourself if the product is still good value to your target market. If the answer is Yes, you have a good mail order proposition.

Your First Step

Nobody can guarantee you anything in mail order. The most experienced professionals will sometimes fail—and fail badly. Your product may be as desirable as ice cream in an oasis, inexpensive as sand on the shore, novel as a portable hole and the market may still reject it. Thus your first step in any direct mail venture should be *testing*.

This is not a beginner's approach: it is the approach you should—must—adopt throughout your entire direct mail career. However well you think you know the market, however well you think you know your product, the *only* way to be certain is to test.

Testing works like this:

Your potential target market may be, let's say, 1,000,000 people. If the unit cost of your mailing pack is only £1, you will invest a million to reach your market—and that is a lot of risk money by any criterion.

If, however, you mail only 1,000 out of that million, you obviously risk substantially less. But what is even more interesting is that the percentage response you achieve on the smaller mailing will almost always match the response you will achieve on a full-scale roll-out within a margin of error of plus or minus 10 per cent.

This is a statistical reality, *not* a guarantee. Most times your roll-out will follow the pattern established in your test, but I have lived through disasters where it did nothing of the sort. There is usually a reason—some change in market dynamics—but this is small consolation when you have just lost your life savings.

But if a test is no guarantee of success, it is a very clear and absolute indication of failure. *If you cannot get a reasonable return on a small-scale test, you will not get reasonable returns on a full-scale roll-out, however much money you spend.* Thus the test becomes a valuable insurance policy which, while it can never guarantee you will make money, will absolutely guarantee to minimize your losses.

Likely Response

Not long ago, I had an interesting discussion with a businessman who was poised to embark on his first direct mail project. As a positive thinker, he was extremely optimistic about its profit potential. He had done his calculations and figured he needed only a 32 per cent sale response to break even. Everything after that was gravy. He was stunned when I told him his chances of achieving a 32 per cent sale response were only marginally better than his chances of being struck down by a meteorite on his way home from work.

Inexperienced marketeers frequently overestimate the response levels in a direct mail exercise. And those few who bother to research the subject beforehand all too often fail to compare like with like.

A mail order project may solicit a direct purchase or a request for further information. It may offer a product on approval or a subsidiary product free. It may require a charitable donation or an information-based response. Each of these *types* of direct mail exercise will typically generate a different response level.

Offers of literature or additional information will generate a higher response than an attempt to sell product direct. So will product on approval or deferred payment schemes. The highest response level of all, in my personal experience, was generated by a request for information. A magazine publisher sought to discover why former subscribers had discontinued their subscriptions and mailed a cross-section of them with a questionnaire. Very much to my surprise, he achieved a 62 per cent response—a figure which may well be a world record. Even free offers do not usually achieve anything like this result, since human greed is to some extent overcome by human suspicion.

When you attempt to evaluate the probable response to a direct purchase offer, cost can be a determining factor. Common sense is an excellent guide here: it is fairly obvious that you will always sell fewer diamond necklaces at a unit price of £100,000 than copper bracelets guaranteed to cure rheumatism at a unit price of £1.50.

So presuming you have a median cost product which you want to sell direct in a single stage operation, what level of response can you reasonably expect?

Given a good list and a good mailing, you should not be disappointed if you expect a 3 per cent response.

That is not a misprint. The figure is 3 per cent, not 30 per cent; and even then it presupposes a good list and a good mailing package. Your *actual* response may be higher—I have had experience of offers which generated 10 per cent, 12 per cent and, on one remarkable occasion, 18 per cent—but don't bank on it. When you are doing advance calculations, base them on a 3 per cent response and if this does not make you sufficient money, then forget the project.

How to Calculate Break-even

Every direct mail project has a magic level where the income finally balances the outgoings: the break-even point. Once this point has been achieved, every extra penny that comes in is profit. Calculating your break-even is not particularly difficult, but you do need to be thorough.

First, you need to decide on the composition of your solicitation package. A fairly typical solicitation might consist of:

1. Outer envelope.
2. Colour brochure.
3. Cover letter.
4. Order form.
5. Reply-paid envelope.

Some mailings comprise a great many more elements, of course, with separate special offer flyers, coupons and so on. Oddly, the more elements in a mailing package, the more response it tends to pull and I have happily created 18-piece mailings for clients who needed them. Even this is by no means large: last year my office received a 42-piece mailing and I doubt if this is anywhere near the top limit. But the number of items included in your mailing must be related to cost and consequently it is important to know which items are really important.

Of the five items previously listed, the outer envelope is obviously an absolute necessity since it carries all the rest. But what of the remainder?

Research shows that response increases when you make it easy for your prospect to take action. Anything, however small, which acts as a barrier against action dampens response. A reply-paid envelope increases response since it means your target does not have to find a postage stamp. But a reply-paid envelope also costs, and over several thousands of a mailing, that cost can mount up. If you decide against a reply-paid envelope on cost grounds, consider the inclusion of a self-addressed envelope. This will also increase response (although not so much as reply-paid) and is obviously cheaper. If you have to pare costs to the bone, forget the envelope altogether: it's desirable, but not completely necessary.

Most marketeers are sold on the idea of a colour brochure or similar print piece in their mailing, and it is definitely a good idea if you can afford it. But if you can't, don't worry: two-colour or even black-and-white print material can be equally effective providing it is well written and acceptably designed.

Believe it or not, you can even drop the print material completely and generate a successful response from the cover letter! Research has shown time and time again that a well-written letter will always beat a brochure in terms of direct response.

There is a reason for this. Unlike mainstream advertising, the selling power of direct mail is vested almost completely in the *written word*. Design, graphics, half-tones and the rest exist in a mailing *only to support the written word* not, usually, as sales generators in their own right. A letter/brochure combination is powerful and should be your goal if at all possible. But if you *must* drop one of the two, drop the brochure. Your letter, properly drafted, will continue to sell without it.

The Order Form should not be dropped. The whole reason for your mailing is to persuade prospects to buy and the Order Form is the vehicle by which they will buy. You may incorporate it in your brochure. You may incorporate it in your letter. Or you may enclose it separately. But don't forget it.

Having decided on the content of your mailing, you are then in a position to begin your break-even calculations. Work on the basis of a thousand units to begin with. This is a good size for a test and later, when you mail a higher volume, you will benefit from economies of scale and your figures will look even sweeter. But for now, work out what it will cost you to produce 1,000 mailing packs comprising the outer envelopes, cover letter, order form and whatever else you have decided to include.

Next, calculate postage. This may actually turn out to be a little less costly than you might imagine. Many post offices, including those of Great Britain and the Republic of Ireland, are anxious to encourage direct mail and will consequently offer bulk mailing discounts. Rather than giving you information which might well be outdated by the time you read this, I would suggest you contact your local post office to find out what is currently on offer. Make sure to ask if any schemes are in operation for first-time mailings.

If you are not physically putting together your mailing pack yourself, you will face an additional cost per item to fund those who will do it for you. Add this to your postage and production and you have the overall cost per thousand of your solicitation mailing.

Next work out your *gross* profit per order. This is the *margin* I mentioned earlier, the difference between your manufacturing or purchase costs and your selling price. From this, deduct any fulfilment cost which is not covered by your selling price. (This may be postage, or packaging, or some far more esoteric item like special warehousing, insurance or whatever.) Assume a maximum 3 per cent return, which is thirty orders generated by your 1,000 mailing. Multiply up and you will have the total projected return per thousand of your mailing.

If this does not cover your costs and make you at least a small profit, forget the whole thing and start again.

Like most generalized rules, there are exceptions to this one. Some mail order propositions can withstand an initial loss, provided sufficient continuity can be built into the exercise to recoup this and make a profit later. Many mail order book clubs provide examples of this technique. You've probably seen their advertising offering a selection of expensive books for a token payment when you join the club. If you have ever wondered how this sort of offer could be made to pay, the answer is that it cannot—at least not in itself. But the loss sustained in the initial offer is more than balanced by the *ongoing* revenue each new customer represents.

Another possibility for converting a losing mailing into a winner is a back-up offer with an exceptionally high margin. You might, for example, be prepared to sustain a loss on an original offer of a book on computers provided you were in a position to make money later by selling respondents computer supplies.

Another exception to the basic rule arises where your original offer is a product which in itself creates the need for additional purchases. Polaroid cameras are an interesting example. These cameras require a special film, only manufactured by the Polaroid Corporation. Thus your purchase of a Polaroid camera automatically generates an ongoing need for Polaroid film. In such circumstances, a loss may be taken on the camera in the confident expectation that it will eventually be covered by profits on the film.

But while there are exceptions, you would be well advised to ignore them until you have become a skilled mail order practitioner. Make your estimate and if it does not show a profit, forget it. Trying to claw back a disaster through continuity sales or second offers is a mug's name for a beginner.

If your estimate looks good, run your test. And if *that* doesn't turn a profit, forget it. Only when the estimate looks good should you move on to a test. Only when the test turns out good should you move on to a roll-out.

And before we leave the subject of mail order, you might be interested in a few tips on how to maximize your chances of your mailing making good.

11
THE SELLING SECRET

There is a trick to writing good advertising copy. The same trick may be used to evaluate it, to create telling business letters, to negotiate successful contracts, even, if you are so minded, to sell brushes door to door.

The trick is this: *Put yourself in the other person's place.*

If you take nothing else away from this book, take those seven words. They contain the secret of successful selling, whatever your business, whatever your marketing method. They deserve to be engraved in stone, put up in lights, or at the very least inscribed on a small plaque which you might someday keep on your highly-polished desk as a reminder of the one piece of advice that made you rich.

Like many another important insight, this one is so simple that it is frequently overlooked; and might even be misunderstood. But it is so vital to your plans for getting rich that I propose to devote this entire chapter to demonstrating its uses.

Writing Business Letters That Work

Since our last chapter was on mailings, let's begin with something relevant to that exercise—but nothing so ambitious as the creation of a mailing pack letter or brochure. Let's start instead with something really fundamental, really simple—a straightforward business letter; the sort of thing you might send out any day of the week. Here's one developed by a major incentive promotions company and mailed in the hope of interesting the chairman of an advertising agency in their wares:

Dear Sir/Madam,

We are an international public company specializing in developing sales promotion programmes based upon complimentary holiday accommodation in Ireland, the UK and Europe.

We are highly successful and have several major clients such as . . . (*Here followed quite an impressive client listing*).

A number of our promotional programmes have been developed in collaboration with promotion houses and advertising agencies with whom we agree a fee structure.

I would like to come and see you to discuss a promotion in greater detail, so I will telephone you to arrange a mutually convenient appointment.

Yours sincerely

Not a lot wrong with that letter you might say. It's short, succinct, businesslike and states its case clearly. And in truth, it is not the worst business letter I have ever read. But like most business letters, it is composed from the viewpoint of the writer, not the reader.

That letter was written with two definite goals in mind. It was designed to interest the reader in the writer's service and it sought to clear the way for a face-to-face meeting. How much more effectively would both these objectives have been achieved if the writer had only tried to *put himself in the other person's place*.

Dear Mr Lalor,

Your clients rely on you for cost-effective, workable, exciting and unusual promotional ideas—and this is an area where my company can be of enormous help to you.

We specialize in sales promotion programmes based on free (yes, free!) holiday accommodation in Ireland, the UK and Europe. In the past, we have had very happy working relationships with advertising agencies similar to your own—relationships which have made considerable profits for both parties.

I feel sure you will want to learn more about what we have to offer and since I know you are an extremely busy man, I have prepared a brief (fifteen minute) presentation which I would like to show you in your office. May I ring your secretary for an appointment?

Yours sincerely

P.S. You may want to check out our operation in advance. If so, I can refer you to (*Here we would add the client list*) all of whom have been valued clients.

If you examine both versions of the letter, you will notice they are virtually identical in terms of *information*. Where they differ dramatically is *presentation*.

The Power of Names

Version 2 begins by using the reader's *name*. Names are important to people. Members of primitive cultures consider a name so important that they often keep it secret, believing that to know a person's name gives you power over him. This is a belief I share, having proven its validity time and time again in direct response advertising. Even today in the most sophisticated cultures, names are magic. Nothing sounds so sweet to you as your own name; which is precisely why successful salespeople tend to use it frequently.

But Version 1 of the letter did not use the recipient's name, did not even trouble to find out his sex. Consciously or not, the reader must feel a little slighted; or at best feel he might be the recipient of a circular rather than a personal letter. By putting himself in the reader's place, the writer would have realized there was something lacking in his original salutation and might have done something about it.

In the first paragraph of Version 1, the writer launched right in about his company and his service. This is exactly the way a thousand similar business letters have begun; and every one of them has failed to achieve maximum impact because of it.

If you are in business, it is only natural that you should wake up in the morning thinking about your company, your product. They are, after all, a major concern in your life, the source of your income and, quite possibly, your major satisfaction.

But however important your company and your product are to you, they mean nothing at all to me. I have problems of my own: my wife who does not love me . . . my children who will not obey me . . . my boss who does not appreciate me. I wrestle with the problems of middle age: falling hair and failing sexuality. I worry about shortness of breath and those strange recurring pains in my chest. I look beyond my imminent retirement and begin to wonder about the great spectre of my own death.

And while all this is going on in my head, you and many another business person is tugging at my sleeve and saying, 'Hey, Herbie, why don't you buy my brand of cornflakes? . . . 'Hey, Herbie, wouldn't you like to drive the sort of car I sell? . . . 'Hey, Herbie, how about coming to my pool hall tonight?'

Linking Your Appeal

Put in that context, you can see you haven't got a prayer of attracting my attention. Unless, of course, you link your appeal to one or more of my personal concerns . . . and that means *putting yourself in my place*.

In Version 2 of the letter, an attempt was made to stand in the reader's shoes right from the very first paragraph. It is not difficult to imagine that the chairman of an advertising agency might be concerned about keeping his clients happy. Thus we linked what we had to sell with this personal concern and, hopefully, attracted his attention from the moment he began to read.

The second paragraph of Version 2 continues to see things from the reader's viewpoint, reassuring him that others in his position have taken up the offer and profited substantially from it.

The third paragraph acknowledges that the reader is busy and, in doing so, makes it easy for him to accept an interview (knowing it will be brief) and difficult to refuse (since he would have to instruct his secretary to put a stop to it).

The postscript introduces the writer's client list in a manner that is again linked to the reader's concerns—this time for certainty and security. (Postscripts, incidentally, are the most frequently read parts of any direct mail package, so make sure yours contains something important.)

Overall, the simple strategy of *putting yourself in the other person's place* produced a far more effective business letter than the original attempt which simply followed standard business practice. Strongly *selling* letters—such as might form part of a mailing package—may be created in exactly the same way. So can brochures, flyers, advertising of all kinds. You may not have what the advertising industry terms *creativity*. You may not be able to write very well or design professional-looking layouts. But the chances are that if you *put yourself in the other person's place* the advertising you create will be far more effective than material which may look twice as good and read twice as well, but still refuses to see things from the reader's viewpoint.

Creating Advertising That Works

According to some research that landed on my desk the other day, readers spend an average of four seconds on a newspaper page. That is not a misprint. The average time spent is four *seconds*.

The figure is slightly less incredible if you stop to think how you read a newspaper. Certainly you read it very differently from the way you read a book. You do not, for example, start up there at the top left hand corner and read quietly through to the end. Instead you *glance at the headlines*. If something interests you, you may read on: at least as far as the end of the opening paragraph. If nothing catches your attention, you turn the page.

When you go into business and begin to spend money on advertising, it is chastening to realize that you have *four seconds* to make your expensive advertising work for you, four seconds to reach out from the page and grab your reader's attention. But at least that realization teaches you the importance of the headline, which is about all that is going to be read in the time allocated. If your headline is weak, the rest of your advertisement will not matter, because it will not get read.

Professionals in advertising often spend a great deal of time—and charge a great deal of money—developing clever headlines. A colleague of mine once developed the cleverest headline I have ever read. The illustration on the ad showed the back of a car. The headline read: THE BOOT WITH A CLEAN PAIR OF HEELS. He was, of course, suggesting very cleverly that this was a fast car. But like far too many in the business, he failed to *put himself in his reader's place*.

Readers may be mildly interested in clever headlines. They may read them and admire them. But they do not *respond* to them. A reader will *only* respond to something which links to his personal concerns, which promises a benefit. The promise does not need to be made cleverly, only clearly. Charles Atlas, the bodybuilder, ran a photo of himself in his ads and promised YOU TOO CAN HAVE A BODY LIKE MINE. There was nothing clever about that headline, but it worked. Joe Karbo, the American author, developed a headline which said MAKE $500 THIS WEEKEND, GUARANTEED. Nothing clever about that either, but it sold 170,000 copies of his book in a single year—at $10 a copy.

Both these headlines linked their promise to reader concerns. Men, particularly young men, are interested in looking good. Most of them believe a muscular body to be a sexual asset. Thus the promise of a body like that of Charles Atlas (who was voted 'The World's Most Perfectly Developed Man') had enormous appeal. Everybody wants more money, so the promise of $500 come the weekend is extremely potent—and was even more so in the early 1970s when Karbo first made it and $500 was worth a great deal more than it is today.

When you develop the promise in your ad, keep putting yourself in the reader's place as you write the body copy. You know all about the product you have to offer from your own viewpoint. Now try to see it from the buyer's viewpoint. Figure out how it will benefit—and pack your copy with those benefits from the very first paragraph. Don't worry about length: it is a fallacy that only short advertising sells. (In fact there is a growing body of research to suggest the very opposite is true, although length will never sell on its own unless you have the knack of *putting yourself in the reader's place*). Keep writing until you have spelled out all the benefits, then tell them how, where and when they can buy and how much it will cost them. This is a ludicrously simple formula which will, if properly applied, bring you in more business than you can handle.

How to Sell Face to Face

The application of precisely the same principle (*Put yourself in the other person's place*) will help you sell effectively face to face. It will also help you select your best prospects more efficiently—no mean trick in itself.

By putting yourself in the other persons's place you can quickly decide whether your prospect has any need for your product; and if so, how the need manifests. Teenagers have little need of vacuum cleaners, for example: they prefer to live in squalor, as you have probably realized if you have teenage children of your own. The more mature individual is a much more likely prospect for this type of product, but putting yourself in the other person's place will show you that the homeminder needs your product to clean the house while the breadwinner may be far more interested in using it to clean the car.

The sort of information you extract by putting yourself in the other person's place is invaluable in selling. It allows you to link the benefits of your product to their personal concerns and to select the sort of examples and demonstrations which are of real relevance.

Nor should putting yourself in the other person's place be based solely on judgement and imagination. When you are selling by mail or media advertising, judgement and imagination are just about all you have, along with market research and, eventually, experience. But in selling face to face, you may have the co-operation of the other person as well, if you play your cards right.

At one stage of my career, I earned a living selling face to face. My product was an extremely expensive weight loss course. Prospective clients were attracted to the clinic by advertising which promised a free consultation. These consultations were carried out by a team of salespeople which included myself. I have to tell you in all modesty that my success rate in selling courses was more than treble that of any other salesperson.

Needless to say, this situation quickly attracted the attention of my colleagues, who would often sit in on my selling sessions in an attempt to discover the secret of my selling pitch. They soon discovered—with a real measure of confusion—that I did not have a selling pitch. I talked to every prospective client differently. Worse still, for long periods I did not talk at all.

In fact, as you will certainly have guessed, the real secret lies in that last sentence, because I kept quiet in order to let my prospective clients talk. And while they talked, I listened and interjected only occasionally in order to encourage them to tell me their personal concerns.

People are only too willing to tell their personal concerns to anyone who exhibits genuine interest and sympathy. Thus I would quickly learn one prospect wanted to lose weight because her marriage was going on the rocks, another was worried about his health, another simply wanted to fit into her best dress for an important occasion. And so on. Once I knew where their concerns lay, I was able to tell them how our particular course could help them. I never thought of this as a 'sales pitch', but the overall technique of discovering a prospect's needs then demonstrating how the course could satisfy him, proved one of the most potent ways of selling courses the clinic ever discovered.

Exactly the same technique will work in every other form of face-to-face selling, however sophisticated. It will work for products as diverse as floor brushes and computers. And it will work because however sophisticated the product, it is always bought by and almost always used by human beings. Since my days in the clinic, I have used exactly the same technique to sell medical equipment with a unit price in excess of a quarter of a million pounds. My colleagues referred to what I did as 'selling to hospitals'. I knew from long experience I was selling to people and tried each time to *put myself in the buyer's place*.

How to Negotiate a Contract

It is my view that selling, in one form or another, is 90 per cent of a successful business. But there are other aspects which are important too. Personnel management is one. Negotiation is another.

It should be fairly obvious by now how valuable the ability to put yourself in the other person's place will be in the art of personnel management. As an employee, you can well remember how poorly your employer understood you. When you go into business for yourself and, hopefully expand sufficiently to employ others to do the hard work, putting yourself in the other person's place will help you avoid that particular mistake completely. There is a political theory that many wars break out because the protagonists did not understand each other sufficiently well to avoid them. Whether or not this is true, there is little doubt that failures in understanding contribute dramatically to the incidence of industrial disputes.

You can avoid disputes of this type by putting yourself in the other person's place—preferably *before* the trouble starts. The effort you expend to do so will cost you a little time. A major misunderstanding with your employees could cost you your company.

Putting yourself in the other person's place will enable you to see your organization *as it is viewed by the people who work within it*. This viewpoint is often dramatically different from your own. I can recall a newspaper group where I once worked which embodied dissociated viewpoints to an almost unbelievable degree. On one occasion the major directors disappeared from their offices for almost two weeks. I later discovered they were on a fund-raising operation on which the entire future of the group depended. At much the same time, they had decided against another potential solution to the crisis: a take-over bid which would have left each of them personally wealthy. The reason for refusing the bid was that it did not include job security for the staff, whose welfare, the directors felt, should take precedence over their own.

This then was the situation from the directors' viewpoint. The employees, by contrast, felt the bosses had gone missing for two weeks in order to go on a drinking binge.

If the divergent viewpoint appears extreme, it is as well to mention that the directors, while fighting to save the jobs of their employees, were so removed from putting themselves in the other person's place that they did not realize the employees themselves were both willing and able to raise the money necessary to save the group. The story had, in fact, a happy ending; but more by luck than good judgement.

If the art of putting yourself in the other person's place is important in personnel management, it is absolutely vital in negotiations.

A few years ago, the senior directors of a company with which I was associated, decided that one of the Board members—an executive director who had been with the company since its foundation—had become redundant. Without consultation with any other colleagues on the Board, they invited her to a private meeting and told her so. They then presented her with what they considered to be a fair and reasonable redundancy package.

Predictably, she blew up in their faces—except that her reaction was not predictable to businessmen incapable of putting themselves in someone else's place. Worse still, remaining Board members (who had not been consulted on the matter until the damage was done) became extremely angry. Within a week, a situation which might have been arranged amicably became a matter for negotiation between lawyers. The eventual outcome was such a swingeing claim against the company that the major shareholder and managing director was forced to sell out inside the year.

Putting yourself in the other person's place allows you to avoid crudities of this type. But far more importantly, it allows you to incorporate subtleties into your own negotiating stance. You are not only privy to understanding the other person's case, but you can evaluate the strength of your own stance by looking at it from the other person's point of view.

It may appear tortuous to have devoted an entire chapter to a single rule of business. Yet this rule is so far-reaching, so important that it will contribute far more to your personal success story than any other.

Putting yourself in your customer's place (with brutal honesty) will allow you to evaluate the viability and worth of your product, the strength of your back-up service.

Putting youself in a potential customer's place will permit you to develop or evaluate your advertising correctly.

Putting yourself in your employees' place will help you

avoid those situations which lead to dispute, and should, if you are willing to act on your insights, permit you to increase productivity beyond your corporate rivals.

Putting yourself in your partner's place will allow you to structure your business for maximum mutual returns—and ensure full, friendly co-operation when you need it most.

In short, *putting yourself in the other person's place* is the single most important secret of business success.

12
SETTING UP YOUR OWN MONEY MACHINE

Now you have learned how to chose the sort of business that will suit you best and have even learned the secret of making it succeed, it is time to learn (perhaps a little belatedly) how to set it up. The peculiar sequence is, in fact, deliberate. As you will see, many of the things you have already learned will be invaluable to you in the establishment of your own Money Machine.

Let's start the ball rolling with OPM.

The Liberating Power of OPM

OPM stands for Other People's Money. And it is OPM you should use when you are setting up your business. There are a number of reasons for this, not least of them being that you probably do not have enough of your own money to set up the business properly.

But the rationale goes beyond that. Anyone using his own money exclusively to set up in business suffers under a distinct psychological disadvantage. You know where the bottom line has to be drawn. You have no failsafe, no fallback position. You have engaged in an exercise analogous to boat-burning and it will almost always make you nervous. There are more than enough things to make you nervous in business without adding to them. Use OPM and relax a litle.

There is, however, more than one type of OPM. It might originate, for example, from a partner, an investor or a bank.

Partnerships have their benefits. They spread the risk and may introduce a degree of expertise you do not personally have. But they also halve the profits and introduce the potential of disagreement.

You are going to have to make up your own mind on the broad question of a partner. But if money is the *only* motivation for bringing in a partner, forget it unless you are truly desperate—and even then think twice. One of the earliest business lessons I ever learned (thankfully, *not* at first hand) was that it is virtually impossible to go into partnership with money and still retain control of your enterprise. However the contracts are negotiated, however the shares are distributed, the fact remains that the person who controls the purse-strings ultimately controls everything. A partner may proved valuable in terms of experience, expertise or ability, but a partner taken on only for the size of his wallet is no longer a partner but a boss.

The same caveat applies to an investor, although it may be applied perhaps a little more cautiously. There *are* investors who are prepared to hand you their money then fade into the background while you get on with the the job. But human nature being what it is, such investors are rare. Most will succumb, sooner or later, to the temptation of interfering. Maybe you can cope with this, but never forget that, like the hypothetical partner discussed above, the investor has control of the purse strings.

Far and away the best form of funding for your new business is a loan. It allows you to invest sufficient money to ensure that the business has a real chance of success (under-capitalization is to businesses as heart disease is to businessmen) while allowing you to retain real control of your destiny. Since loans require to be repaid, this route also forces you to discipline yourself financially right from the start, which is no bad thing.

You have two potential sources for your loan: a private individual or a financial institution. The latter is always preferable to the former, if only because financial institutions do not take it personally if circumstances force you to default. (This is not an unimportant consideration. A friend of mine had to leave the United States after defaulting on a loan. He had borrowed from an individual and, to his profound unease, later discovered the individual was a member of the Mafia.)

Preparing a Presentation

Wherever you decide to borrow, you are going to need something which will persuade your target you do not plan to take the money and run for Bermuda. Specifically, you are going to need the sort of documentation which indicates that the business you plan to start has some chance of success and that, consequently, the loan and its interest are likely to be repaid. Technically, this documentation is known as a *presentation*. I have never been able to understand why it reassures anyone, but experience shows that it does.

Your presentation should indicate the nature of your proposed business, how it will be structured, where it will operate, its target market and how much it will cost to set up. Precision is everything. It is useless to suggest the business will require a capital investment of somewhere between £20,000 and £30,000. Lenders are unimpressed by this sort of woolliness: they require a document that assures them the launch will require £25,792.78. They will also require to know *how much of this money you are going to put up yourself and how you plan to secure the loan*.

You now know why I suggested earlier in this book that you begin your rags-to-riches career by getting yourself a job. It is the job—and a little conscientious saving—which will fund your percentage of the investment. And it is your job which will make the possibility of a loan feasible in the first place: there are few individuals or institutions advertising loans to the unemployed.

The amount you are prepared to invest of your own money

is relatively unimportant, so long as you are prepared to invest *something*. Do not fall into the trap of investing too heavily. It will make little enough *real* difference to the way your loan application is viewed, and it could make a lot of difference to your personal financial circumstances. Resist demands for security if you can. Such demands are often no more than a reflex action on the part of the lender. If you are in employment and prepared to personally guarantee repayment, you should get your money (if you persevere) without hocking your house or your spouse.

Alongside the facts and figures already mentioned, your presentation will have to include what are known as *projections*. These are detailed figures showing what sort of profits you expect to make over a given time span: usually not less than one year and not more than three. Most presentations are optimistic in their forecasts and there is absolutely no reason why you should be overcome by a rush of honesty in this respect.

The simplest and in many ways the most effective and impressive way to put together a presentation of this type is to turn the whole thing over to an accountant. Your accountant will organize the documentation and often agree to come with you while you make the presentation. Some accountants will actually undertake to raise the loan for you—a service which is usually well worth the fee they charge.

If you elect to prepare the presentation yourself, remember that appearance is important. Your documentation should be neatly typed, mistake-free (especially in the sections containing figures) and neatly bound. You will need more than one copy since you will be required to leave at least one—and possibly more—with the lender for study.

The curious thing about presentations of this sort is that ultimately their precision is quite worthless. No one knows exactly how much he is going to need to float a business. He might make an educated guess about the ballpark, but precision will only come with experience *after* the business is set up. Projections are even more ludicrous. Actual sales depend on 1001 factors, most of which are outside your control: competitive activity, economic fluctuations, market reaction, seasonality and so on. Projections are guesswork, often undertaken with no better motive than keeping a banker happy. An accountant's projections reek of certainty and professionalism, but beneath the veneer they are simply figures based on your guesswork.

But, silly though the whole exercise may seem, it is also necessary. When you take steps to float a loan, it is a game you will have to play, so make sure you play it to the best of your ability.

The Miracle Power of Pictures

However well you prepare your presentation, however optimistic and impressive your figures, there is no guarantee you will get your loan. It is a sad fact of business that there are far more people with a need to borrow than with a need to lend. In order to ensure you find yourself among the happy few who actually receive the cash, you need to apply the miracle power of pictures.

The sort of loan application we're discussing is a form of *selling*. Specifically, you are selling somebody on the success of a business that does not yet exist. And because you are engaged in a form of selling, you can successfully apply selling techniques.

In the last chapter, I told you about the most important sales technique of all: the ability to *put yourself in the other person's place*. Right next to that technique in importance comes the one I want to introduce you to now: the ability to *paint pictures inside the human head*.

By painting pictures inside somebody's head, I mean stimulating their imagination—not in any generalized way, but specifically. In a career that has embraced selling in a variety of forms, I long ago discovered that the sale is really made the moment your prospect begins to *visualize*.

The visual imagination is a magical and marvellous thing. Properly manipulated it becomes a dynamo which drives emotions: and emotions, in turn, determine what we buy.

If you are ever tempted towards the fallacy that people make purchases on the basis of common sense and logic, think on the humble bicycle. The bicycle is a marvellous invention: the most efficient conversion of energy to motion human ingenuity has yet developed. As a mode of transportation it is economical to buy, free to run, non-polluting and healthy. The motor car is none of these things, yet car sales worldwide far outstrip the sales of bicycles. The average car is built to transport a minimun of four people, but usually transports only one—its driver. It consumes irreplaceable, fossil fuel, pollutes the atmosphere, requires costly roadways and contributes not one whit to our health and fitness. But we aspire to bigger and better cars as status symbols, sex substitutes or whatever. Logic? You must be joking!

If you are selling someone a dishwasher, it is useless embarking on the technical details of the machine. As every successful salesperson knows, the thing to do is concentrate on the *benefits*. But (putting yourself in the other person's place) the benefits must be related to your prospects. They have to be told how the new dishwasher will make life easier for them. And they have to be told in such a way that they start to imagine the way they could live if only they owned that dishwasher. The more vividly you can persuade them to visualize, the more likely they are to buy.

What they are visualizing often has little enough to do with the dishwasher. They may see themselves reading a book, relaxing in front of the TV, having a drink, digging the garden or whatever. The dishwasher is there in the background, chugging away at the washing-up and creating extra time for them to do the things they want to do. But the internal cinema show they are viewing is selling them that dishwasher just the same.

That's the pictures in the head; and that is a technique which will work even in a situation where there is no immediate benefit (and quite possibly no benefit at all) to the individual who owns the head. I do not know why this works, only that it does. As you describe the business you are about to launch, paint pictures in the mind of your bankers. Once they begin to *see* your business in their mind's eye, they become far more likely to float the loan you need.

The Tycoon Dilemmas

This book is subtitled *A Beginner's Manual*. In it, I have attempted to show you the steps you need to take in order to set your feet firmly on the road to riches. How far you follow that road is obviously up to you, and the problems which may arise as the result of wealth lie outside the scope of the present work. All the same, I cannot quite resist the temptation to discuss briefly, some of the more commonplace of the Tycoon Dilemmas you are likely to face, because while having money is infinitely preferable to poverty, it does generate its own high-class problems.

The first common problem is not, strictly speaking, generated by wealth, but rather by the route to wealth I have advocated in this book. Running your own business is frightening, worrying, ulcer-generating and, despite everything, a whole heap of fun. For a great many people business is a way of life, an addiction, the most important source of gratification in their lives. For a sizeable percentage of such people, business becomes of greater importance than money or marriage.

Before you reach that extreme stage, you are likely to face the first of the Tycoon Dilemmas: the choice between expansion and profit.

Profit is the money that accrues after you have paid off your debts, your running costs, your salaries and your taxes. Profit is money you can bank, spend, invest—or plough back into your business. It is that final possibility that is the interesting one. Reinvesting your profits leads (usually) to expanded business. Expanded business leads to increased profits—or so the theory goes. But the reality is that expanded business doesn't always lead to increased profits. Sometimes it just leads to expanded business.

I have watched this happen more than once. An individual founds a business in the hope of getting rich. The motivation for getting rich is usually expressed as a desire to experience the good life, to live in a bigger house, drive a more comfortable car, run a Lear jet or two and perhaps indulge in such vulgarities as solid gold bath taps. But as the business grows and more and more wealth is generated, the individual does none of these things. Instead he (and it almost always is *he*) becomes captivated by an increasingly large and complex game. He spends more and more time, more and more *money* on creating a bigger and more powerful business empire.

There is, of course, absolutely nothing wrong with this. How you spend your money is your affair and if you get more pleasure out of running a multi-national than you would out of lounging in the sun, that is nobody's business but your own. The only reason I brought it up here is that far too often the decision to become a super tycoon is never actually made: it simply *happens*. You start out seeking wealth, but somewhere along the line your goalposts move and you find yourself increasingly shooting for power, prestige and success, which are not the same thing at all. So when the first Tycoon Dilemma—profit or expansion?—comes your way, make sure you take the decision *consciously* and select the road that promises you the most *personal* satisfaction.

The second Tycoon Dilemma is in some respects similar to the first: it is the choice between fun and money.

Most people seek money with a set of unspoken and largely unexamined assumptions. They assume money will buy them comfort, security and, if not happiness, at least a bit of fun. Such assumptions are *almost* correct: money *can* buy all these things, but whether or not it *will* buy any of them is strictly up to you.

For some, making money gradually and very subtly becomes an *end in itself*. The Dickensian character of Scrooge is an archetype, the characteristics of which are a cliché precisely because they are so readily encountered.

It is, thankfully, unlikely that you will end up as a tramp shuffling around the doss-houses with half a million pounds stuffed into a brown paper bag. But it is entirely possible that you will end up the sort of businessperson who works twenty hours a day not for the power and prestige of running a large organization, not in the hope of earning enough to buy a second mansion in Florida, but rather for the sterile accumulation of zeros in a bank account.

Whatever you feel about abandoning your earlier ambitions in order to pursue power and prestige, anyone working to earn money as an end in itself requires, in my opinion, to use some of that cash to hire a good psychiatrist.

Founding a business, forming a company, is like giving birth. You create an entity *separate from yourself*. Oddly, many businesspeople—even quite successful businesspeople—never quite realize this. Consequently, they assume that what is good for their business is good for them. Sometimes, of course, they are right, but there is nothing automatic about the process. It is as well to remember that every hour you spend with your business is one less hour spent with your family, is one less hour devoted to art and literature, is one less hour to enjoy the sight of golden corn ripening in the summer sun.

I often feel that any course in business studies should have a section in it devoted to what NOT to do when you get rich. It might contain advice on how to avoid accumulating *useless* money, assets which appear only as figures in a bank's computers. It might discuss the art of personal fulfilment, so that your wealth is not diverted into sterile enterprises.

Perhaps most importantly of all, it should show the way to

genuine self-knowledge so that you can spend your money to achieve the maximum return—but a return not measured in financial terms.

INDEX